Using
Amazon Alexa
and Echo

Michael Miller

Contents

Chapter 1:
Getting to Know Amazon Alexa and Echo

Amazon's Echo and Echo Dot are so-called "smart" speakers that have taken the tech industry—and households across the nation—by storm. These unobtrusive devices use a built-in personal digital assistant, dubbed Alexa, to find information, answer questions, and operate all manner of household devices, all with plain-English voice commands.

What is Alexa?

The success of Amazon's Echo devices is due primarily to the voice and artificial intelligence behind the scenes. Alexa is that voice and AI; she is what (or who?) you interact with, and drives virtually everything that your Echo does.

Of course, Alexa isn't a real human being. She's just a disembodied voice driven by a piece of software, residing in the cloud and speaking (and listening) through your Echo device. You interact with Alexa with voice commands—that is, you talk to her and she talks back. There are no keyboards or touchscreens to tap (aside from the Echo Show device, that is). All your interactions with Alexa are vocal.

If you've ever used Siri on an Apple iPhone or iPad (or, for that matter, Cortana on a Windows 10 PC), Alexa will be familiar to you. (It's also similar to the Google Assistant found on the competing Google Home smart speaker.) You talk to your Echo device to ask Alexa a question or issue a command, and Alexa answers your question or does what you've asked it to do. You speak, Alexa listens. Alexa "speaks," and you get whatever it is you've asked for.

What kinds of things can you use Alexa to do? Your imagination is the limit. You can ask her to read current information (news headlines, weather conditions and forecasts, sports scores), find interesting and useful facts, calculate math problems and perform all manner of conversions, and even retrieve and read back recipes. You can use Alexa to play music, read audiobooks, add items to your calendar or to-do list, and order items online. (From Amazon, of course.) You can even use Alexa to control various smart devices in your home, if you're into that. And, not surprisingly, she can even play games.

How Alexa Works

While it might seem that Alexa resides within your Echo device (and she does, in part), her intelligence resides in that part of the Internet we call the *cloud*. That means she has to connect to the Internet, via your home wireless network, to work.

When you ask Alexa a question, she essentially does an Internet search and comes back with the closest answer, which she then reads to you. If you give a command, she searches her database of known commands to perform the action requested. It's a little unnerving if you've never dealt with artificial intelligence; close your eyes, and it's as if you're talking to a human servant instead of a digital one.

All of Alexa's commands and answers are stored in the cloud. General commands are baked into Alexa's own intelligence, but you can make her "smarter" by adding additional *skills*. These are small voice-activated apps that enable Alexa to perform new tasks. At present Alexa has more than 10,000 skills you can enable, with more being developed (by both Amazon and third parties) every day. This way Alexa becomes even more useful over time.

Using Alexa with Amazon's Echo Devices

As noted, Alexa is a piece of AI software. You interface with Alexa via a piece of hardware, a freestanding controller that plugs into the nearest electrical outlet and connects to the Internet via your home's Wi-Fi network.

Amazon offers an entire family of Alexa-controlled devices. These devices—all branching from the original Amazon Echo smart speaker—include wireless connectivity, built-in speakers and microphones, and similar operation. Today you can choose from the original Echo smart speaker, the smaller (and less expensive) Echo Dot, the touchscreen-enabled Echo Show, the webcam-enabled Echo Look, and the portable Amazon Tap.

Members of the Amazon Echo family—the Amazon Echo (in white and black), Echo Dot, and Amazon Tap

Whichever Alexa-enabled device you use, you use it much the same fashion. Connect the device to your home wireless network, link it to your Amazon account and the accompanying Alexa app on your smartphone, and then start talking. It's that simple.

And you're not limited to a single Echo device in your home. Amazon encourages you to purchase multiple Echo devices, so you can put one in each room—living room, bedroom, kitchen, you name it. You can even use your Echo devices to create a multi-room intercom system. (And to voice call friends and family who also have Echo devices in their homes!)

You might think that talking to a houseful of Echo devices would get confusing; what if you speak to the Echo in your living room but the Echo in your kitchen also hears you? Well, Amazon thought of that, and incorporates Echo Spatial Perception (ESP) technology to ensure that only the device closest to you will respond to your commands. Nifty!

How Alexa—and the Echo—Came to Be

You probably know Amazon as the world's largest online retailer, selling books, music, movies, and just about everything online at www.amazon.com. But Amazon is also a big player in the technology space, hosting servers that rent space to all manner of online companies, as well as developing various hardware devices, such as the Kindle book reader, Fire tablet, Fire TV box, and Fire TV Stick. It's this tech-forward environment that led to the launch of Alexa and Echo.

The Echo was originally envisioned as an intelligent voice-controlled appliance that could play music, read aloud news and weather reports, and order groceries and other good. Development on the Echo started in 2011, and at the time there was nothing like it.

To pull together Echo and the Alexa voice control system, Amazon's engineers had to work with multiple cutting edge technologies. We're talking voice recognition, text-to-speech, cloud computing, wireless networking, smart devices, and more. It took several years (and a few outside acquisitions) to pull it all together, but Amazon finally released the initial Echo in November of 2014. The Echo Dot followed in March, 2016, with a second generation Dot in October of that year. Today Amazon sells a half-dozen Echo devices, licenses Alexa technology to dozens of other companies for use in their devices, and owns 75% of the fast-growing market for smart speakers/controllers. And all this from a company that started as a simple online bookstore!

Chapter 2:
Choosing the Right Amazon Echo Device

The Alexa personal digital assistant is built into many different devices. The first of these was the Amazon Echo smart speaker, quickly followed by other devices in the Echo line—the smaller, more affordable Echo Dot, the touchscreen-enabled Echo Show, the webcam-enabled Echo Look, and the battery-operated Amazon Tap. (Okay, that last one didn't have the word "Echo" in its name, but it's clearly part of the same line.) Amazon also builds Alexa capability into its line of Fire TV devices as well as its Fire tablets. And now there are a multitude of third-party devices that license Alexa technology from Amazon, from smart TVs to smart thermostats to smart baby monitors.

In other words, you can get Alexa functionality in just about any type of device you want. But which configuration is best for your personal needs?

Amazon Echo

The Amazon Echo is the original Alexa-enabled device. Devised and originally sold as a so-called "smart speaker," the Echo is all that and more – and remains Amazon's best-selling Alexa-enabled device.

The Echo is indeed a speaker that you can use to listen not just to Alexa's responses but also music, streamed over the Internet. As such it includes a 2.5" woofer and a 2" tweeter for what Amazon calls "immersive 360-degree omni-directional audio." It has the best sound of any of Amazon's Echo devices, but it's more like a table radio than an audiophile sound system.

The Echo includes seven built-in microphones and incorporates special beam-forming technology for far-field voice recognition. That means that the Echo can hear your voice, speaking at a normal volume, from across the room—even when music or your TV is playing.

The original Amazon Echo smart speaker

Like other devices in the Echo family, the main Echo comes with both Wi-Fi and Bluetooth wireless connectivity built in. You can use Bluetooth to connect to other speakers or audio sources; the Wi-Fi connectivity is for connecting to other smart devices via your home wireless network.

The Echo unit is taller than other devices in the Echo family, due to the dual speakers and accompanying reflex port that improves its bass response. It's a cylinder that's 9.25" tall and 3.3" in diameter, with four push buttons on top. It comes in either black or white, and sells for $179.99. Like all of Amazon's devices, it can be purchased at www.amazon.com.

Echo Dot

Amazon recognized that not everyone used the Echo for listening to music—and that many people desired a lower-cost alternative to the full-sized Echo. Hence the introduction of the Echo Dot, now in its second generation. The Dot is a more compact version of the larger Echo device, with a single, smaller speaker, no bass reflex port, and a lower price point—just $49.99. At that price, you can buy three Dots and have some change left over from what you'd spend on a single Echo. (The price also contributes to the fact that the Echo Dot is not only the best-selling device in the Echo line, but also Amazon's top-selling tech device, period.)

Amazon's small and affordable Echo Dot

Aside from the difference in speakers, the Echo Dot does everything the original Echo does. It has the same Bluetooth and Wi-Fi connectivity of its larger sibling, as well as the same seven-microphone array. It's voice controlled and the built-in speaker can be used both to listen to Alexa's responses and to listen to music. (It just doesn't sound as good as the larger Echo device; if you want better sound, connect it to an external speaker via the included audio jack or wirelessly with Bluetooth.)

As to specifications, the Echo Dot comes in at just 1.3" tall and 3.3" wide. It looks a little like a hockey puck or a drink coaster, and is definitely less conspicuous than the original Echo when sitting on your living room table.

Echo Show

The latest member in Amazon's Echo family is the Echo Show. The Show is an Echo device with 7" touchscreen—or, thinking of it another way, a 7" touchscreen with Alexa capability built in. In any case, you get all the functionality of Alexa with the added benefit of being able to see its responses onscreen.

Naturally, the Echo Show features the same Wi-Fi and Bluetooth wireless capabilities found in other Echo devices, as well as multi-microphone voice control. It has dual 2" speakers for front-firing stereo sound.

Amazon's Echo Show with touchscreen display

The Echo Show's touchscreen adds some nice functionality to Alexa's traditional voice control and response. The screen can display video clips as part of your Flash Briefing; show weather conditions and forecasts onscreen; display your calendar and to-do lists; function as a digital photo frame with picture slideshows; display feeds from security cameras, baby monitors, and doorbell cams; and show recipe ingredients and instructions while you're cooking. You can also use the Echo Show to conduct video chats with other Echo Show users.

This added functionality comes at a price. The Echo Show is the most expensive device in Amazon's Echo line, coming in at $229.99. It's available in either black or white cases. The unit is a 7.4" square frame that sits 3.5" deep.

Echo Look

The Echo Look is a niche device that adds a selfie cam to the normal Echo features. (Amazon calls it a "hands-free camera and style assistant.") It's designed for people who want to see how they look and assess their style.

You use the Echo Look to take full-length photos and short videos of yourself in various articles of clothing. Use Alexa's voice controls to shoot the pics and vids; just say "**Alexa, take a picture**" or "**Alexa, take a video**." The Look's depth-sensing camera includes built-in LED lighting and applies an automatic background blur effect to help you look your best, whatever you're wearing.

Amazon's Echo Look hands-free camera (and style assistant)

Since the Echo Look has full Alexa capability (including microphones and speaker) built-in, you can also use it to do just about anything the more traditional Echo devices can do. It also includes a Style Check function, where you submit photos of two outfits and get expert advice back as to which looks best on you. And, not surprisingly, the Echo Look is designed to make shopping for clothes (on Amazon.com, of course) as convenient as possible.

The Echo Look is a small and stylish device, measuring 6.3" tall and 2.4" in diameter. It comes with a tripod base so you can set it and forget it; the depth-sensing camera has 5MP resolution. It sells for $199.99.

Amazon Tap

If you want all the functionality of an Amazon Echo device but in a fully portable form factor, check out the Amazon Tap. Even though it isn't called an Echo, it is; the Tap is essential a battery-powered, portable smart speaker. (You don't have to use it on battery power, however; you can also plug it into a standard wall outlet for power.)

The Amazon Tap portable Bluetooth smart speaker

As such, the Tap is great if you want to take a smart speaker with you out on the porch or deck, when go you camping or boating, or just to shuffle a single speaker with you from room to room. The Tap connects to your main audio system via Bluetooth, or streams tunes from Amazon Music when it's connected to your Wi-Fi network. In terms of voice commands, it does everything the AC-powered Echo does, it's just portable.

Size-wise, the Tap is a little smaller than the Echo, at 6.3" tall and 2.6" in diameter. Sound-wise, it isn't quite as good as the traditional Echo; it features smaller dual 1.5" speakers and dual passive radiators. Naturally, the Tap includes built-in microphones for voice control and supports both Bluetooth and Wi-Fi connectivity. It sells for $129.99.

Fire TV

Alexa voice-control functionality is built into Amazon's Fire TV, a Roku-like streaming media player that lets you watch a variety of programming on your living room or bedroom TV. Just connect the Fire TV box to your TV and choose from a large number of streaming audio and video options, including Netflix, Hulu, Amazon Video, and more.

The Fire TV set-top box and Voice Remote

Because Alexa voice-control is built in, you can completely control the Fire TV box without using the traditional remote control. Just say "**Alexa, launch Netflix**" or "**Alexa, play *Game of Thrones***" and Fire TV will fire up the designated programming. Naturally, the Fire TV box can also do all the other Alexa-related things that Amazon's Echo devices do.

The Fire TV connects via HDMI to just about any modern television set. Unlike Echo devices, Fire TV doesn't have a built-in microphone; instead, you speak into the device's Voice Remote. (It also doesn't have built-in speakers; the sound plays through your TV.) The Fire TV box sells for $89.99.

Fire TV Stick

Amazon's Fire TV Stick offers all the functionality of the Fire TV box, but in a smaller, dongle-like design that plugs directly into your TV's HDMI port. You can use Alexa to choose and control your programming, and to do normal Alexa-type stuff. You control Alexa via the included Voice Remote. At $39.99, the Fire TV Stick is the most affordable Alexa-enabled device available today.

Amazon's Fire TV Stick and Voice Remote

Fire Tablet

Amazon includes Alexa functionality with pretty much all of its hardware devices. Case in point is the Fire Tablet, Amazon's Android-based answer to Apple's iPad. The Fire Tablet is fully Alexa enabled, which means you can ask it the same types of questions as you do a more traditional Echo device. Think of Alexa on the Fire Tablet like Siri on the iPad; your own personal digital assistant.

Amazon's Fire Tablet with Alexa included, in a variety of colors

Amazon offers Fire Tablets in a variety of configurations, starting at $49.99.

Dash Wand

Amazon's Dash Wand is an interesting little device with a single purpose— to help you buy more stuff from Amazon.com. It's essentially a bar code reader with limited Alexa functionality built-in. You wave the Dash Wand over the item you want to order or re-order, and it automatically sends that order to Amazon. You can also talk to it and have Alexa place an order for what you want. For example, say "**Alexa, paper towels**" and the Dash Wand sends an order for paper towels to the mothership.

Because of the Alexa functionality, you can also use the Dash Wand to search for recipes, perform conversions, and even find nearby restaurants. It's not as full-featured as the other Alexa-enabled devices, but it does what it's designed to do. The Dash Wand sells for $20, but Amazon typically offers a $20 credit on your next purchase, so it's kind of free. If you need that sort of thing.

Amazon's Dash Wand, with limited Alexa functionality

Third-Party Devices

In addition to including Alexa in its own Echo and Fire devices, Amazon has licensed Alexa technology to a variety of other companies, to incorporate in their own smart devices. Alexa is now built-in to a variety of other products, from smart speakers and baby monitors to smart thermostats and smart TVs. Let's look at what's available, as of summer 2017. (Expect more third-party Alexa-enabled products to be introduced as time goes by.)

Aristotle Smart Child Monitor

Nabi's Aristotle is a combination baby monitor, Wi-Fi security camera, and Bluetooth speaker, all controlled via voice commands. It also includes Alexa functionality, so you can control it via Alexa commands—as well as do all other Alexa-related stuff. Say "Alexa" to access normal Alexa functions, or "Aristotle" for all the kid-friendly stuff. Expect this to sell for $349 when it's released. Learn more at www.nabitablet.com/aristotle.

Bixi

The current Bixi model is an innovative remote control for smart home devices that works via hand gestures. Parent company Bluemint Labs plans to introduce a second generation model later in 2017 that adds Alexa voice control to Bixi's current gesture controls. Learn more at www.bixi.io.

COWIN DiDa Speaker

COWIN's DiDa is a Bluetooth portable speaker with Alexa built in—kind of like the Amazon Echo, but with slightly better sound quality. You get dual 7.5-watt drivers in a compact black design, along with a rechargeable battery. It sells for $99.99; learn more at www.cowinaudio.com.

ecobee4 Smart Thermostat

If you're at all interested in smart thermostats, this is the way to go. The ecobee4 is the latest model in ecobee's family of intelligent controllers, utilizing the company's innovative room sensors to help minimize hot or cold smarts throughout your house. This new model adds Alexa voice control so you can control your heating/cooling by saying "**Alexa, turn up the heat**" or whatever. Plus it includes full Alexa functionality, so you don't need an Echo in the same room to do all your Alexa stuff. At $249, it's cheaper than buying another smart thermostat and separate Echo device. Learn more at www.ecobee.com.

The ecobee4 smart thermostat with Alexa control

Element Amazon Fire TV Edition TVs

Element manufactures a full range of smart TVs, and some of them come with Amazon's Fire TV system built-in. These Element Fire TVs also include Alexa functionality, so you can control the TV via voice commands—as well as do anything else Alexa-related. The newest Element Fire TVs are 4K models for the best picture quality, and are budget priced—selling from $450 (for a 43" model) to $900 (for a 65" model). Learn more at www.elementelectronics.com.

FABRIQ Smart Speaker

Here's another Echo competitor, the FABRIQ Smart Speaker. It's just like an Echo, a freestanding speaker with Alexa functionality built-in. The FABRIQ is smaller than the Echo, offers with two 2" drivers and 5 watts of power, and runs on either AC or battery power for portable operation. (It also comes in a unique fabric covering.) What's nice about this one is the price; at $49.99 you get better Echo-quality sound at an Echo Dot price. Learn more at www.thefabriq.com.

GE Sol Lamp

GE's Sol is an innovative freestanding LED light that incorporates Alexa functionality. You can control the Sol lamp with Alexa voice commands, or ask Alexa anything else via the lamp. It's due for release later in 2017. Learn more at www.cbyge.com/pages/sol.

GE's innovative Sol lamp with Alexa functionality built-in

Hugo Smart Camera

Hubble's Hugo is a smart camera with built-in functionality. It's particularly popular as a child monitor, as Alexa lets your children interact with the device while they're being monitored. Hugo will be released later in 2017; learn more at www.hubbleconnected.com/hugo.

iLuv Aud Click Wi-Fi Speaker

The Aud Click is a portable Wi-Fi/Bluetooth speaker with built-in Alexa functionality. It runs on either AC or battery power, and sells for just $49.99. Learn more at www.iluv.com/products/audclick.

Lenovo Smart Assistant

Lenovo, the PC manufacturer, plans to release its own smart speaker later in 2017. Dubbed the Smart Assistant, it looks a little like an Amazon Echo and has Alexa functionality built in. Learn more at www3.lenovo.com/us/en/new-products/Lenovo-Smart-Assistant/ p/99SD9EI1SA1.

LG InstaView Refrigerator

How about a smart refrigerator with Alexa voice commands build in? That's what LG offers in its InstaView fridge, along with a 29" translucent touchscreen in the refrigerator door. Use Alexa to search for recipes, add ingredients to a shopping list, place food orders from Amazon.com, play music, display the weather forecast, and control all your other smart home devices. Learn more at www.lg.com/us/discover/instaview-door-in-door.

Logitech ZeroTouch

Logitech's ZeroTouch lets you bring Alexa to your car. It's a car phone holder that incorporates Alexa voice control and functionality (through the Alexa app on your phone). It's available for Android phones only, priced from $59.99. Learn more at www.logitech.com/en-us/ product/zerotouch-car-phone-holder.

Nucleus Intercom System

The Nucleus is a whole-house video intercom system with touchscreen displays and Alexa functionality. Check up on who's doing what in which room, then ask Alexa to do whatever else you want. Individual units sell for $140; learn more at www.nucleuslife.com.

Omaker WoW Speaker

Omaker's WoW speaker is a handsfree wireless (Wi-Fi and Bluetooth) speaker with Alex functionality included. It includes dual 4-watt speakers and runs on either AC or battery power. It sells for $169 but is often discounted to around $100. Learn more at www.eomaker.com/omaker-wow-wireless-wifi-portable-bluetooth-speakers-with-amazon-alexa.html.

TCL Xess Home Hub

TCL's Xess is a little like a big Amazon Echo Show. It's a smart home controller built into a 17.3" HD display, with a separate remote security camera. Alexa functionality is built in, and you can also use it to watch movies and TV shows. It's expensive, at $499.99, but think of it more as a big Android tablet with Alexa built in.

Triby Smart Speaker

Triby is a portable wireless speaker with Alexa functionality built-in. It includes two speakers and a passive radiator for big sound in an otherwise smallish device. It also includes a small e-ink display for leaving notes to other family members. Triby sells for $199; learn more at www.invoxia.com/triby/.

The Triby smart portable speaker

Vobot Smart Clock

Vobot is a smart alarm clock with Alexa functionality included. Just tell it when you want to wake up, and it does the rest. It should sell for around $35 when its released later in 2017; learn more at www.getvobot.com/clock.

Westinghouse Amazon Fire TV Edition TVs

Just like Element (discussed previously), Westinghouse also offers a range of smart TVs with Amazon's Fire TV service built-in. And where there's Fire (TV), there's Alexa. Use the included remote control to speak your commands and control your TV, as well as do all the expected Alexa-related stuff. Prices range from $449 for a 43" model to $899 for a 65" set. Learn more at the www.westinghouseelectronics.com/products/ website.

Which is the Right Alexa-Enabled Device for You?

With all the different Amazon Echo models available—as well as an increasing number of third-party products with Alexa built-in—which Alexa-enabled controller is right for your specific needs?

Here are my recommendations:

- If you want to listen to music in addition to using Alexa skills, go with the original Amazon Echo or one of the many competing Alexa-enabled smart speakers.
- If you don't listen to as much music and/or you're on a budget, go with the lower-priced Amazon Echo Dot.
- If you want to use your device purely for smart home control, also go with the Echo Dot.
- If you want smart home control and are also in the market for a smart thermostat, buy the ecobee4.
- If you want Alexa control and are also in the market for a new living room or bedroom TV, consider one of the Amazon Fire TV Edition sets from Element or Westinghouse.
- If you want Alexa control and are also in the market for a streaming media player, go with the Fire TV box or Fire TV Stick.

- If you want to use Alexa to replace your bedroom alarm clock, go with the forthcoming Vobot smart clock or Amazon Echo Show with touchscreen display.
- If you want Alexa functionality in the kitchen, for recipes and videos and such, go with the Amazon Echo Show with touchscreen display.
- If you want to partake in Alexa-enabled video calls with friends and family, buy the Amazon Echo Show with touchscreen display.

I'll make it even simpler. For most of us the Echo Dot is the best choice. (It is Amazon's best-selling Echo device, after all.) The Dot is inexpensive and unobtrusive, and it does everything the larger (and more expensive) Echo does. And it's cheap enough that you can buy several to use throughout your home!

Chapter 3:
Setting Up Your Echo Device

Whatever type of Echo device you have, the setup and operation is identical. When you first take your device out of the box, you need to connect it to your home Wi-Fi network, download the Alexa app to your smartphone or tablet, and then pair your Echo with the smartphone app. After that, you can configure a handful of settings to make your Echo device work better for you.

Initial Setup

Everything physical you need to set up your Echo device is included in the box. That means the Echo device itself and a power cord. Beyond that, you'll need to use your smartphone or tablet to go online to your device's app store and download the Amazon Alexa app. (It's free.) With that done, it's time to get started with the setup.

Before you get too far, however, note that your Echo device needs to be connected to your Amazon account to take advantage of all the information and content in your account. If you purchased your device direct from Amazon, it will be preloaded with your account information. If you purchased the device elsewhere, you'll need to log into your Amazon account from the Alexa smartphone app when prompted during the initial setup process.

1. Connect one end of the power cable to the Echo, and the other to a nearby power outlet.
2. Launch the Alexa app on your smartphone or tablet.
3. The Alexa app should recognize you from your Amazon account. (If it doesn't, follow the onscreen instructions to sign into your account.) Tap **Begin Setup**.
4. Tap to select the type device you're setting up.
5. On the next screen, select your language (if it isn't English), then tap **Continue**.

Connecting an Echo Dot to a power source

6. Make sure your smartphone or tablet is connected to your home Wi-Fi network, then tap **Connect to Wi-Fi**.
7. When your Echo is ready to connect, Alexa will tell you so and the ring on the top of the device will turn orange. When this happens, tap **Continue**.

Getting ready to connect

8. Your smartphone now tries to pair with your Echo. When the connection is established, tap **Continue**.

9. You now see a list of available Wi-Fi networks. Tap to select your network from the list. (Make sure the network you choose is the same one to which your smartphone is connected.)

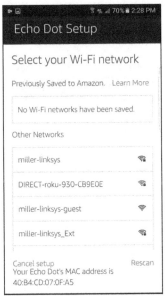

Choosing your home Wi-Fi network

10. Enter the password for your network into the **Password** box.

11. To save this password, so you don't have to enter it every time you launch the app, tap **Save password to Amazon**.

12. Tap **Connect**.

13. Amazon now prepares your Echo for initial use. This may take a few minutes and involve downloading the latest updates.

14. When the setup is complete, tap **Continue**.

15. If you're connecting an Echo Dot, you'll be prompted how you want to use the device—with a Bluetooth speaker, with an external speaker via audio cable, or with no additional speakers. Make your selection.

16. You may be prompted to view a short video about your Echo. Do so if you wish, or tap your phone's back button to exit out of this.

17. You now see the Alexa app's home screen. You're ready to start using your Echo!

Navigating the Alexa Mobile App

While you work with Alexa via voice commands on your Echo device, you do most of the configuration of Alexa via the Alexa smartphone app.

As you'll quickly see, the Alexa app is relatively simple and easy to use, and you won't need to use it much. But it's good to know what's there and why and how to use it, if you need to. To that end, let's launch the Alexa app and take a short tour.

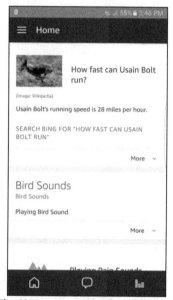

The Home screen in the Alexa app

1. Tap the **Home** icon to display the Home screen, which displays cards that reflect commands and activities that Alexa has completed, the latest first. Scroll down to view additional cards.

2. If you've been playing music on your Echo device, a now playing pane may appear at the bottom of the screen. Tap the **Play** button to resume playback, or tap the **Volume** button to change the volume level.

3. For some cards, Alexa would like to know how well she performed. If Alexa heard you right, tap **Yes**. If Alexa had a problem, tap **No**. Alternatively, tap **Less** to not display this section.

The Conversations screen

4. Tap the **Conversations** icon to display the Conversations screen, which displays past conversations with other Alexa users and lets you start new ones. Tap **Contacts** icon to view other friends who have Alexa-enabled devices; tap the **Start Conversation** icon to start a conversation with anther Alexa user.

5. Tap the **Now Playing** icon to display the Now Playing screen. From here you can control playback of items you've played through your Echo, view items in the queue, and view recently played items (History).

The Alexa app's Now Playing screen

6. From any screen, tap the **Menu** (three-bar) button to display the left navigation panel.

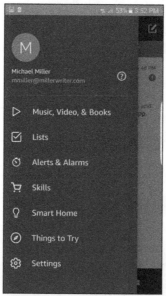

The Menu (navigation) pane in the Alexa app.

7. Tap **Music, Video, & Books** to view details about and control specific music, book, and video (on an Echo Show) services connected to your Alexa account.
8. Tap **Lists** to view and edit your shopping and to-do lists.
9. Tap **Alerts & Alarms** to manage the reminders, alarms, and timers.
10. Tap **Skills** to view and add new skills to Alexa.
11. Tap **Smart Home** to view and control smart devices with Alexa.
12. Tap **Things to Try** to get suggestions of fun and useful things you can do with Alexa.
13. Tap Settings to view and configure additional Alexa settings.

Using Echo's Buttons

The Amazon Echo and Echo Dot devices have physical buttons on the top that perform specific functions. The buttons differ between the Echo and the Dot.

The Echo Dot has four buttons:

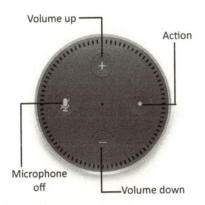

- **Volume up**: Increases the volume level.
- **Volume down**: Decreases the volume level.
- **Action**: Performs different functions depending on what Alexa is doing. When a timer or alarm is set, press this button to turn off the timer or alarm. When your device is asleep, press this button to wake it up. And if you want to connect your device to a Wi-Fi network, press and hold until the light ring turns orange.

- **Microphone off**: Press this button to turn off the device's microphones; press again to turn the microphones back on

The large Amazon Echo device has only two buttons on the top, Action and Microphone off. With the Echo, you increase the volume level by turning the Volume ring (on the outside edge of the device, beneath the light ring) clockwise, or decrease the volume level by turning the Volume ring counterclockwise.

Decoding Echo's Colors

Echo's outside ring (called, not surprisingly, the light ring) lights up in a variety of colors, depending on what it's doing. It's a good idea to learn what each color means, to better use your Echo device.

Color/Status	Description
All lights off	Echo is active and waiting for your commands
Solid blue with spinning cyan lights	Echo is starting up
Solid blue with cyan pointing in direction of person speaking	Alexa is processing your request/command
Orange light spinning clockwise	Echo is connecting to your Wi-Fi network.
Solid red light	Echo is muted and microphones are disabled
White light	You are adjusting the device's volume level
Continuous oscillating violet light	There was an error during Wi-Fi setup; wait a few minutes or try again
Spinning blue light that ends in a solid purple light	Do Not Disturb mode is enabled
Single flash of purple light after an interaction with Alexa	Do Not Disturb is active

Color/Status	Description
Pulsing yellow light	A message or notification is waiting for you; to retrieve your messages, say "**Alexa, play my messages**"
Pulsing green light	Your Echo is receiving an incoming call; say "**Alexa, answer**" to answer the call or "**Alexa, ignore**" to ignore the call

Chapter 4:
Personalizing Your Echo Device

There are many settings you can configure to personalize your Echo to work better for your own individual needs. You can change the wake word from "Alexa" to something more user-friendly; you can link your Alexa device to other music, calendar, and list accounts you use; you can even add other users to your Echo, so that everyone in your home can have a personalized experience.

Changing the Wake Word

Let's start with the "wake word" you use to activate Alexa. By default, this wake word is "Alexa." So, for example, if you wanted to know today's weather forecast, you would say **"Alexa, what's the weather today**?" If you don't say the wake word (for example, if you simply say **"What's the weather today?"**), your Echo doesn't wake up and Alexa doesn't hear you.

Why the word "Alexa?" There are two main reasons. First, Alexa is a relatively uncommon word; saying most other words might falsely trigger the device. (Imagine if the wake word was "Bob" or "cheese" or "Trump.") The second reason is that the "x" in "Alexa" is a hard consonant that is recognized with greater precision than other letters—it simply works better than most other words.

Alternate Wake Words

What if you don't like the wake word "Alexa?" What if your daughter's name is Alexa and you get tired of your Echo activated every time someone calls her by name? What if you just want to wake up your Echo with something cooler?

Whatever your reasons, Amazon enables you to change your Echo's wake word. You can choose from four different words:

- Alexa
- Amazon
- Echo
- Computer

By the way, that last wake word is a gift to Star Trek fans. Every crewmember on Starship *Enterprise* interfaces with the ship's computer by first saying, "Computer." In fact, if you want to have a little fun, change Alexa's wake word to "computer" and ask your Echo "**Computer, beam me up**" or "**Computer, tea, Earl Grey, hot**." Fun stuff, there.

Select a Different Wake Word
So how do you change the wake word for your Echo device? Follow these steps:

1. From the Home screen of the Alexa app, tap the **Menu** (three-bar) button to display the left navigation pane.
2. Tap **Settings** to display the Settings screen.
3. In the Devices section at the top of the screen, tap your Echo device.
4. Scroll down to the General section and tap **Wake Word**.
5. On the Change Your Wake Word screen, tap the down arrow in the first list box.
6. Tap to select your desired wake word.
7. Tap **Save**. You will now be able to wake your Echo with your new wake word.

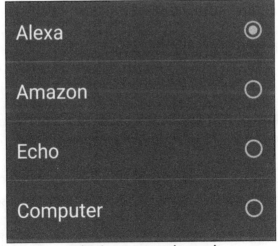

Selecting a new wake word

Linking Accounts from Other Services

Alexa gets more powerful when you link her to other services that you use. You can link Alexa to your accounts with streaming music services, online calendars, and online to-do lists.

Follow these steps:

1. From within the Alexa app, tap the **Menu** button to display the left navigation panel.
2. Tap **Settings** to display the Settings screen.
3. Scroll to the Accounts section and tap **Music & Media**.
4. Go to the account you want to add to Alexa, then tap **Link account**.
5. If you already have an account with this service, tap the **Log In** button or link and then follow the onscreen instructions to log into and link to this account.
6. If you don't yet have an account with this service, tap the **Sign Up** button or link and then follow the onscreen instructions to create a new account.
7. Return to the Settings screen, scroll to the Accounts section, and then tap **Calendar**.
8. Tap the tile for the calendar you'd like to use with Alexa.
9. Tap **Link your calendar account to** link this account, then follow any additional onscreen instructions to log onto your calendar account and complete the process.
10. If you want to link to a third party to-do list service, in addition to the lists feature built-into Alexa, return to the Settings screen, scroll to the Accounts section, and then tap **Lists**.
11. Tap **Link** for the to-do list account you want to link to, then follow the onscreen instructions to complete the process.

Setting Up Multiple Users

Here's something else you can do if you have a busy household. If you have multiple people with their own Amazon accounts using your Echo, you can link all of these accounts to your Echo, so that you can access your spouse's to-do list or your kids can play your music playlists. All you have to do is set up multiple users in the Alexa app.

Add a New User

To be set up as a user for your Echo, each person needs to have their own Amazon account. (This precludes setting up young children as users— unless they're also Amazon purchasers with their own accounts.) You'll need the Amazon username/email address and password of each person you want to add.

Follow these steps:

1. From within the Alexa app, tap the **Menu** button to display the left navigation panel.
2. Tap **Settings** to display the Settings screen.
3. Scroll to the Accounts section and tap **Household Profile**. This displays the Invite a Household Member screen.
4. Tap **Start**.
5. Hand your smartphone to the person you want to add as a user, then have them press **OK**.
6. Have this person enter their email address (or phone, for mobile accounts) and Amazon password, then tap **Verify Account**.
7. Get your phone back from the other person, then you both can use Alexa on your Echo device.

Adding a new user to your Echo

Work with Multiple Users

When you've set up multiple users for your Echo, you can each other's music, books, and other content. You can also collaborate on shopping lists, to-do lists, and calendars.

With multiple accounts, not only can you share your content libraries, such as books and music. You can also collaborate on stuff like shopping lists, to-do lists and calendars.

To access another user's content, you have to switch to that person's account. Just say:

"Alexa, switch accounts" *or*

"Alexa, switch to [Bob's] profile"

To see which account is currently active, say:

"Alexa, which account is this" *or*

"Alexa, which profile am I using?"

Remove a User from Your Echo

If you'd prefer *not* to have a specific person linked to your Echo, you can remove that person. Follow these steps:

1. From within the Alexa app, tap the **Menu** button.
2. Tap **Settings** to display the Settings screen.
3. Scroll to the Accounts section and tap **Household Profile**.
4. All current users are listed here. Find the person you want to remove and select **Remove** next to their name.
5. Select **Remove from Household** to confirm the change.

Configuring Other Device Options

There are many other settings you can configure to get the most out of Alexa and your Echo device. Most of these settings are just fine in their default configuration, but you can make adjustments as necessary.

To configure device options, tap the **Menu** (three bar) icon then select **Settings**. You now see the options listed in the following sections. Make whatever changes you deem necessary.

Device Settings

All of your Echo devices are listed in the Devices section. Tap a device to configure the following settings:

Setting	Description
Update Wi-Fi	Resets the Wi-Fi network for your Echo device
Bluetooth	Use to pair a new Bluetooth device with your Echo
Pair Device Remote	Use to pair a remote control for those Fire devices that use a voice remote
Do Not Disturb	Activates Do Not Disturb mode, where your Echo quits listening during specified hours
Scheduled	Sets those hours the Echo "sleeps" when Do Not Disturb mode is activated
Drop In	Manages Drop In functionality for calling other Echo devices; you can opt to turn it on or off or call devices only in your household
Sounds	Choose sounds and adjust volume for Echo system sounds; also turns on or off notification sounds
Device Name	Change the name assigned to this Echo device
Device Location	Edit the location of this device for weather and other local features
Device Time Zone	Sets the time zone for your device
Wake Word	Lets you change the device's wake word from Alexa to Amazon, Echo, or Computer
Temperature Units	Sets Fahrenheit or Celsius
Distance Units	Sets metric or feet/mile measurements
Device is Registered To	Displays the device's owner; you can also opt to deregister the device

Setting	Description
Wi-Fi Networks Saved to Amazon	Explains why Amazon says its safe for you to save your Wi-Fi password to your Amazon account
Device Software Version	Displays the current software version used on this device
Serial Number	Displays the device's serial number
MAC Address	Displays the device's MAC address

You can also tap **Set Up a New Device** to set up a new Echo device.

Accounts Settings

In this section you find a variety of settings that have to do with the various accounts relating to your Echo device, as detailed in this table:

Setting	Description
Notifications	Turns off or on various system notifications
Music & Media	Links various streaming music accounts to Alexa
Flash Briefing	Configures content for your daily Flash Briefing
Sports Update	Selects which teams to follow in your Sports Update
Traffic	Sets your home and work address for traffic reports
Calendar	Links various calendar accounts to Alexa
Lists	Links various to-do list accounts to Alexa
Voice Training	Helps you "train" Alexa to better understand your voice
Voice Purchasing	Sets a four-digit code you have to enter to confirm voice purchases through Amazon.com
Household Profile	Adds other user accounts to Alexa

General Settings

The General section lets you view your device history, sign out of your account, and more.

Setting	Description
History	Displays all your voice interactions with Alexa
About the Amazon Alexa App	Displays key information about the Alexa app
Sign Out	Signs out of the Alexa app on your mobile device

Chapter 5:
Working with Alexa Voice Commands

Alexa responds to your voice commands. All you have to do is ask Alexa a question or give her a command, and she'll provide the answer or perform the task at hand.

Talking to Alexa

Talking to Alexa is as easy as talking to an actual human being. You just need to get her attention, and then tell her what you want. You speak in plain English phrases; use a clear, distinct voice and try not to slur your words. (It also helps if there isn't a lot of background noise in the room; Alexa can't distinguish between different speakers, and sometimes responds to words spoken on the TV or radio!)

You start each question or command with the wake word "Alexa," followed by whatever it is you want Alexa to do, like this:

"Alexa, what's the weather?

"Alexa, turn up the sound."

"Alexa, turn off the living room lights."

"Alexa, how far is it to the moon?"

When Alexa hears the wake word, the ring on the top of the device lights blue, with a small cyan area pointing in the direction of whomever spoke. Alexa listens to your request, and then (sometimes after "thinking" about it for a few seconds) voices her response.

The blue light "points" to the person talking

If Alexa knows the answer to a question, she speaks it. If she doesn't know the answer, she'll tell you. And when you're telling her to do something, she'll provide feedback that the task is done ("Okay"). If she doesn't understand a command, she'll tell you that, too; you can always repeat or rephrase your question or command if necessary.

As you'll quickly learn, Alexa doesn't know (or even understand) everything you can ask of her. There are many questions you can ask that she won't know the answer to. If that's the case, she'll tell you. She'll also tell you if she just didn't understand the question; when this happens, try stating the command again, or maybe try saying it a different way.

Learning General Commands

We'll deal with a lot of topic-specific commands throughout the rest of this book, but let's first look at those general commands that apply across all actions and applications.

When you're using Alexa, you can do the following:

Alexa command	Does this
Alexa, stop *or* Alexa, cancel	Stops (cancels) the current operation
Alexa, pause	Pauses the current operation

Alexa command	Does this
Alexa, mute	Mutes the sound
Alexa, unmute	Unmutes the sound
Alexa, volume five *or* Alexa, volume level five	Sets the volume level; use a number between 0 and 10
Alexa, louder *or* Alexa, turn it up *or* Alexa, turn up the sound	Raises the volume
Alexa, softer *or* Alexa, turn it down *or* Alexa, turn down the volume	Lowers the volume
Alexa, repeat	Repeats what Alexa just said
Alexa, help	Requests assistance with the current operation
Alexa, pair	Puts the Echo into pairing mode for connecting Bluetooth speakers and other devices
Alexa, connect [device name]	Connects to a previously paired Bluetooth device
Alexa, switch accounts	Switches to a different Alexa profile
Alexa, which profile is this?	Checks which profile is currently active

Reviewing Your Echo's History

Your Echo device is constantly listening to what's going on in the room, so it will know when you're giving it a command. This audio is recorded and stored, however briefly, which means you can easily review a history of what Alexa hears.

To view (and listen to) your command history, follow these steps:

1. From within the Alexa smartphone app, tap the **Menu** (three-bar) icon.
2. Tap **Settings** to display the Settings screen.
3. Scroll down to the General section and tap **History**.

4. Everything Alexa has heard is listed here. Tap a particular item to view more details.

5. Tap the **Play** button to hear the audio of this particular command or request.

6. If Alexa did what you wanted, tap **Yes**. If she flubbed it, tap **No**.

7. To delete this voice recording, tap **Delete Voice Recordings**.

Viewing—and replaying—a voice command

Chapter 6:
Getting the Latest News, Weather, Traffic, and Sports

Alexa is great for finding current information. Whether you want to know what's happening out the world stage or whether or not you should wear a raincoat tomorrow, Alexa will tell you.

News Headlines

Let's start with commands related to the latest news. The best way to listen to news headlines is via Alexa's Flash Briefing. This is a personalized news report with stories compiled from your choice of news sources, including the Associated Press, the BBC, NPR, and more. Your Flash Briefing can also contain local weather information from AccuWeather and podcasts from a variety of sources—and, if you have an Echo Show, video clips from your news sources of choice.

Configure Your Flash Briefing

To personalize what you hear in your daily Flash Briefing, follow these steps:

1. Open the Alexa app on your smartphone and tap the **Menu** button.
2. Tap **Settings**.
3. Tap **Flash Briefing**.
4. Tap "on" or "off" various news sources, or tap **Get more Flash Briefing content** to add more content to your briefing.
5. Tap **Edit Order** to change the order in which the briefing content is presented.

Managing Flash Briefing content

News Commands

Once you have your Flash Briefing configured for your personal tastes, it's a simple task to have Alexa read you the latest news.

Alexa command	Does this
Alexa, play my Flash Briefing *or* Alexa, what's the news?	Plays your current Flash Briefing
Alexa, next	Skips to next news story
Alexa, previous	Rereads previous news story
Alexa, pause	Pauses reading the current news story
Alexa, stop *or* Alexa, cancel	Stops playing the Flash Briefing

If you have an Echo Show, you can play a *video* Flash Briefing. You'll see video source options in the Alexa app that you can add to your Flash Briefing; when you're playing your Flash Briefing, tap the screen to display playback options.

Weather Conditions and Forecasts

Alexa uses AccuWeather for all its weather-related information—and there are several ways to ask Alexa about the weather. Try these:

Alexa command	Does this
Alexa, what's the weather?	Reads current weather conditions
Alexa, what's the weather tomorrow?	Reads tomorrow's weather forecast
Alexa, will it rain tomorrow?	Returns rainfall amount from tomorrow's forecast
Alexa, how much snow will we get on [Friday]?	Returns snowfall amount from the specified day's forecast
Alexa, is it going to be sunny on [Wednesday]?	Reads the forecast for the specified day
Alexa, what's the extended forecast?	Reads the extended forecast
Alexa, what's the weather in [San Diego]?	Reads the forecast for the specific location

Sports Scores and News

You can also ask Alexa questions about your favorite sports teams. Alexa includes a Sports Update feature that provides a summary of the latest scores and upcoming games for your favorite teams.

Configure Your Sports Update

To tell Alexa which teams you want to follow in your Sports Update, follow these steps:

1. Open the Alexa app on your smartphone and tap the **Menu** button.
2. Tap **Settings**.
3. Tap **Sports Update**.
4. By default, Alexa has already added the pro sports teams in your area, but you can remove any team by tapping the X.
5. Use the **Search** box to search for additional teams to add.

Managing Sports Update content

Sports Commands

Alexa offers a lot of different ways to find out how your favorite teams are doing. Here are just a few of the available commands.

Alexa command	Does this
Alexa, play my Sports Update	Reads scores and other information about your favorite teams
Alexa, what is the score for the [Bulls] game?	Reads live score for the current game for the specified team
Alexa, what was the score for the [Twins versus Yankees] game?	Reads final score for the specified game
Alexa, did the [Heat] win?	Reads details about the specified team's last game
Alexa, who is winning the [Super Bowl]?	Reads current live score of the specified event
Alexa, who won the [World Series]?	Reads details about the specified event

Alexa command	Does this
Alexa, when do the [Pacers] play next?	Reads next game on the specified team's schedule
Alexa, how are the [Blackhawks] doing?	Reads details of the current team's season

Traffic Information

Then there's traffic. You want to know the best route to a given destination—and whether the route is busy or not? Alexa can tell you.

Set Your Home and Work Addresses

First, though, you have to tell Alexa where you are and where you're going, which you do in the Alexa smartphone app. Follow these steps:

1. From the Alexa app on your smartphone, tap the **Menu** button.
2. Tap **Settings**.
3. Tap **Traffic**.
4. Alexa has prefilled the From section with the address listed on your Amazon account. To change this address, tap **Change address**.
5. In the To section, tap **Add address** to enter your work address.

Traffic Commands

With your location information entered, you can then ask your questions verbally through your Echo device.

Alexa command	Does this
Alexa, how is traffic?	Reads current traffic information
Alexa, how does the commute look?	Reads current traffic information

Chapter 7:
Discovering Useful Information

You're not limited to asking Alexa about the news, weather, wand sports. You can ask Alexa literally anything—and if she knows the answer, she gives it to you. (If she doesn't... well, you're no worse off than you were before, right?)

Asking for Information

You can ask Alexa all sorts of questions. Here are just a few; I'm sure you can think of more!

Alexa command	Does this
Alexa, who is [Steven Spielberg]?	Returns information about person
Alexa, who is [Chief Justice of the Supreme Court]?	Returns answer
Alexa, how far is it from here to [New York City]?	Returns distance
Alexa, how far is it to [the moon]?	Returns distance
Alexa, how tall is the [Empire State Building]?	Returns answer
Alexa, what is the capital of [Brazil]?	Returns answer
Alexa, why is the sky blue?	Returns answer
Alexa, who wrote ["Of Mice and Men?"]	Returns answer
Alexa, what was [Bob Dylan's] first album?	Returns answer
Alexa, who is the lead singer of [Imagine Dragons]?	Returns answer

Alexa command	Does this
Alexa, when did the [American Revolution] take place?	Returns answer about historical event
Alexa, how many people live in [California]?	Returns answer
Alexa, what is the definition of [defenestrate]?	Returns definition
Alexa, how do you spell [Mississippi]?	Spells the word
Alexa, how old is Beyoncé?	Returns answer
Alexa, who plays Superman in "Man of Steel?"	Returns answer
Alexa, who starred in ["The Maltese Falcon"]?	Returns answer
Alexa, what is [George Clooney's] latest movie?	Returns answer
Alexa, what is the IMDb rating for ["Casablanca"]?	Returns answer from IMDb
Alexa, Wikipedia [the solar system] or Alexa, tell me about [the solar system]	Searches Wikipedia for the given topic
Alexa, tell me more (asked after listening to Wikipedia review)	Reads more from the Wikipedia entry

Doing Math

Alexa can calculate all sorts of mathematical equations. She knows the value of all major constants, and can even convert between different units of measurement!

Alexa command	Does this
Alexa, what is 2 plus 4?	Returns answer
Alexa, what is 14 minus 9?	Returns answer
Alexa, what is 5 times 12?	Returns answer
Alexa, what is 27 divided by 3?	Returns answer
Alexa, what is the square root of forty two?	Returns answer
Alexa, how many feet in a mile?	Returns answer
Alexa, how many miles is five kilometers?	Returns conversion
Alexa, how many ounces in a pound?	Returns conversion
Alexa, how many ounces in [three] pounds?	Returns conversion
Alexa, what is the speed of light?	Returns answer
Alexa, what is the value of [pi]?	Returns answer

Playing Games of Chance

You ever need to settle an argument with a coin flip? Or roll a pair of dice in a board game? Well, Alexa can handle all your flipping and rolling—in a completely random and non-biased manner.

Check out these fun commands:

Alexa command	Does this
Alexa, flip a coin	Flips a coin for head or tails
Alexa, heads or tails?	Flips a coin for heads or tails
Alexa, random number between [x] and [y]	Picks a random number between the stated extremes
Alexa, roll a die	Rolls a single die
Alexa, roll [n] [x]-sided dice	Rolls [n] number of dice with [x] number of sides each; for example, to roll two regular cube dice, say **"Alexa, roll two six-sided dice"**

Finding Local Businesses and Events

Want to find a good Indian restaurant near your home? Need to know when your local bakery or drugstore closes? Well, Alexa can help you find all sorts of information about businesses in your area.

Here are some of the things you can ask:

Alexa command	Does this
Alexa, where can I eat lunch?	Lists nearby restaurants
Alexa, what [Thai] restaurants are nearby?	Lists nearby restaurants of the specified type
Alexa, what are some top-rated [sushi] restaurants?	Lists top-rated restaurants of the specified type
Alexa, what [craft stores] are nearby?	Lists nearby businesses of the specified type
Alexa, where are the nearest [office supply stores]?	Lists nearby businesses of the specified type
Alexa, find me a nearby [plumber]	Lists nearby services of the specified type

Alexa command	Does this
Alexa, find the address for [Bob's Vacuum Cleaners]	Reads the address for the specified business
Alexa, find the hours for [Wells Fargo bank]	Reads the hours for the specified business
Alexa, what [pharmacies] are still open?	Lists businesses of the specified type that are currently open
Alexa, what movies are playing nearby?	Lists movies playing in nearby theaters
Alexa, what movies are playing in [Houston] [tomorrow]?	Lists movies playing in a specific location on the specified day
Alexa, what [comedies] are playing [Saturday night]?	Lists movies of the specified type playing in nearby theaters
Alexa, when is ["Casablanca"] playing?	Lists the play times for the specified movie

Chapter 8:
Listening to Music and
Audiobooks

All Echo devices can play back music from your Amazon Music account and other sources. (If you have subscriptions to those services, that is.) While the Echo sounds better, because of its enhanced speakers, the Echo Dot still sounds okay. Just use simple voice commands to play the music you like.

Playing Music

By default, Alexa will play music from your Amazon Music account. (If you don't have one, get one!) You can also listen to music from third-party music streaming services, such as Pandora and Spotify—as well as live radio, podcasts, and shows from iHeartRadio and TuneIn.

Linking Accounts

To listen to music from a third-party provider, you need to have an account with that provider and then link that account to your Alexa account. (The sole exception is TuneIn, which doesn't require an account to listen to.) Here's how to link accounts:

1. From within the Alexa smartphone app, tap the **Menu** button.
2. Tap **Settings**.
3. In the Accounts section, tap **Music & Media**.
4. Tap the **Link Account** link for the music service you want to set up.
5. When prompted, tap **Log In** if you already have an account with this service, or **Sign Up** if you don't yet have an account but want one.
6. Follow the onscreen directions to link or set up an account.

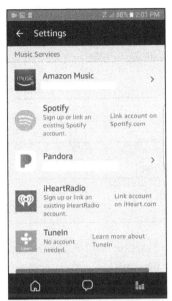

Linking music service accounts

Set Your Default Music Service

By default, the music you ask for is played from Amazon Music. You can change this default service to that your music-related commands are sent to your streaming music service of choice.

1. From within the Alexa smartphone app, tap the **Menu** button.
2. Tap **Settings**.
3. In the Accounts section, tap **Music & Media**.
4. Scroll to the bottom of the screen and tap **Choose Default Music Services**.
5. In the Default Music Library section, accept Amazon Music as your default, or tap **Spotify** to use that service instead.
6. In the Default Station Service section, accept Amazon Music as your default, or tap one of the other services (Pandora or iHeartRadio) to use that service instead.
7. Tap **Done** to save your new defaults.

Music Playback Commands

Whichever music service you like, you can use Alexa to control your music playback. When you issue basic commands, they will be sent to your default music service of choice. (That's Amazon Music, unless you changed it in the previous task.) To send your commands to another streaming service, all you have to do is specify which music service you want to use as part of your command.

Alexa command	Does this
Alexa, play music	Plays random songs
Alexa, play some [classical music]	Plays specified style of music
Alexa, play [children's music]	Plays songs of the specified type
Alexa, play some [Steely Dan]	Plays songs from the specified artist
Alexa, play ["Uptown Funk"]	Plays the specified song
Alexa, play ["Proud Mary"] from ["Creedence Clearwater Revival"]	Plays the specified song from the specified artist
Alexa, play ["Lemonade"]	Plays the specific album
Alexa, play the latest [Adele] album	Plays the specified album
Alexa, play the new song from [Lady Antebellum]	Plays the specific song
Alexa, play the [Top Country] station	Plays the specific station
Alexa, play the top songs this week	Plays the week's most popular songs on Amazon Music
Alexa, play songs with the lyrics ["walk with me"]	Plays songs that contain the specified lyrics
Alexa, play the top [rock] songs from [1995]	Plays the specified songs from the specified year
Alexa, play some [funk] music from the [seventies]	Plays songs of the specified type from the specified era
Alexa, play the top songs from [1980] to [1985]	Plays the top songs from the specified years
Alexa, play some [slow] music	Plays songs that fit the query
Alexa, play some [relaxing] music	Plays songs that fit the query

Alexa command	Does this
Alexa, play some music to help me sleep	Plays a selection of soft music
Alexa, shuffle my [Oldies] playlist	Plays music from the specified playlist, in random order
Alexa, what song is this?	Identifies the currently playing song
Alexa, buy this song	Purchases this song from the Amazon store
Alexa, play the [Yacht Rock Radio] station from [Pandora].	Plays the specific station from the specified provider
Alexa, play [89.3 FM] on [TuneIn]	Plays the specified station on the specified provider
Alexa, play [jazz] from [Spotify]	Plays the specified style of music from the specified provider
Alexa, play [Fox Sports Radio] on [iHeartRadio]	Plays the specified programming from the specified provider
Alexa, I like this song or Alexa, thumbs up	Gives a thumbs up to the current song
Alexa, thumbs down	Gives a thumbs down to the current song
Alexa, louder or Alexa, turn it up or Alexa, turn up the volume	Increases the volume
Alexa, softer or Alexa, turn it down or Alexa, turn down the volume	Decreases the volume
Alexa, mute	Mutes the volume
Alexa, unmute	Unmutes the volume
Alexa, pause	Pauses playback
Alexa, resume	Resumes playback
Alexa, next	Skips to the next song
Alexa, repeat this song	Repeats the current song

Listening to Audiobooks

In addition to listening to music, Alexa lets you listen to audiobooks, read by professional voice talent, from Amazon's Audible service. You can also have Alexa herself read books you've purchased for Amazon's Kindle e-book reader, using the same text-to-speech technology used for Alexa's other voice answers.

Alexa command	Does this
Alexa, read the book [A Farewell to Arms]	Reads the specified Kindle book
Alexa, play audiobook [Catch-22]	Plays the specified audiobook
Alexa, play [Slaughterhouse-Five] from Audible	Plays the specified audiobook
Alexa, pause	Pauses playback
Alexa, resume my book	Resumes playback
Alexa, go forward	Skips forward in the book
Alexa, go back	Skips backward in the book
Alexa, go to the next chapter	Skips to the next chapter in an Audible audiobook
Alexa, go to the previous chapter	Skips to the previous chapter in an Audible audiobook
Alexa, go to chapter [two]	Skips to the specified chapter in an Audible audiobook
Alexa, restart	Restarts reading/playback from the beginning in an Audible audiobook
Alexa, stop reading the book in 30 minutes	Reads the book for the next 30 minutes, then stops (great for reading at bedtime)
Alexa, play the [Science Vs.] podcast	Plays the latest episode of the specified podcast
Alexa, play the previous episode	Plays the previous episode of the current podcast

Chapter 9:
Working with Alarms, Calendars, and Lists

Your Amazon Echo is truly a smart speaker that can do double duty as an alarm clock or timer. Alexa can also help you manage your daily calendar and keep track of items on your shopping and to-do lists.

Telling Time and Date

While most Echo devices (the Echo Show excepted) don't have displays, they can still tell time—and tell you the time via Alexa's voice functionality. All you have to do is ask!

Alexa command	Does this
Alexa, what time is it?	Returns current time
Alexa, what time is it in [London]?	Returns current time in specified city
Alexa, what's the date?	Returns today's date
Alexa, when is [Thanksgiving] this year?	Returns date for specified holiday

Setting an Alarm

Alexa has its own alarm system that you can set using voice commands. Use these commands to set and control an alarm..

Alexa command	Does this
Alexa, wake me up at [seven in the morning]	Sets an alarm
Alexa, set the alarm for [six am]	Sets an alarm
Alexa, set a weekend alarm for [eight am]	Sets an alarm

Alexa command	Does this
Alexa, set a repeating alarm for [Wednesday] at [noon]	Sets an alarm that repeats each week on the given day
Alexa, when is my alarm set for?	Reads alarm details
Alexa, when's my next alarm?	Tells you when the next alarm is set for
Alexa, what alarms are set for tomorrow?	Reads alarm details
Alexa, cancel the alarm for [Wednesday at eight]	Cancels the specified alarm
Alexa, snooze	Enters snooze mode when the alarm goes off
Alexa, stop	Stops the alarm then it goes off

Setting a Timer

Alexa also lets you set timers for specified periods of time. This is great when you need to set a time limit for your kids—or yourself!

Alexa command	Does this
Alexa, set a timer for [twenty minutes]	Sets a timer
Alexa, set a [dinner] timer for [thirty minutes]	Sets a named timer
Alexa, set a second timer for [fifteen] minutes	Sets multiple timers
Alexa, how much time is left on my timer?	Reads the remaining time
Alexa, cancel my timer	Cancels the timer
Alexa, stop	Stops the timer then it goes off

Managing Your Calendar

Alexa can manage online calendars you create with your Google or Outlook.com account. That means you can be notified of events or appointments, as well create new ones via voice command.

Linking Calendars

To use calendars with Alexa, you first have to link your calendar to your Alexa account. Here's how to do it.

1. From within the Alexa smartphone app, tap the **Menu** button.
2. Tap **Settings**.
3. In the Accounts section, tap **Calendar**.
4. Tap the type of calendar you wish to link—Google (Gmail and G Suite), Microsoft (Outlook.com and Office 365), or Apple (iCloud), then follow the onscreen instructions for that particular calendar.
5. In the Alexa Will Add New Events to This Calendar section, tap the down arrow and select which calendar you want Alexa to use by default.

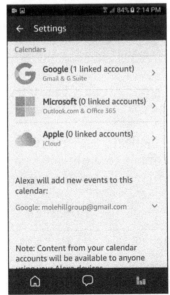

Linking calendars in the Alexa app

Calendar Commands

You can have Alexa tell you about upcoming events on your calendar, as well as add new events.

Alexa command	Does this
Alexa, what's on my calendar?	Lists events for the day
Alexa, what's my next event?	Reads the next upcoming event on your calendar
Alexa, what's on my calendar [Monday]?	Lists events for the specified day
Alexa, what's on my calendar tomorrow [at eleven am]?	Reads any event scheduled at the specified day and time
Alexa, add an event to my calendar	Opens your calendar to add an event; follow the verbal instructions to add details about the event
Alexa, add [lunch meeting] to my calendar for [June 10] at [noon]	Add the specified event to your calendar at the specified day and time

Creating Shopping Lists, To-Do Lists, and Reminders

Alexa includes built-in shopping lists and to-do lists to keep yourself organized. You can add items to each list via voice commands, or view each list in the Alexa app. (Tap the **Menu** button, then tap **Lists**.)

Alexa command	Does this
Alexa, what's on my shopping list?	Lists items on shopping list
Alexa, add [milk] to my shopping list *or* Alexa, I need to buy [milk]	Adds the specified item to your shopping list
Alexa, what's on my to-do list?	Lists items on to-do list
Alexa, create a to-do	Adds a new item to your to-do list

Alexa command	Does this
Alexa, put [weed the garden] on my to-do list	Adds the specified item to your to-do list
Alexa, reminder	Creates a reminder
Alexa, remind me to [check the mail] in [ten minutes}	Creates a specific reminder
Alexa, what reminders do I have [tomorrow]?	Checks reminders on a specific day

Chapter 10:
Discovering Alexa's Easter Eggs

All work and no play makes Alexa a dull girl. Fortunately for her, and for you, there are lots of fun things you can do with Alexa.

Alexa Easter Eggs

Normally when you ask Alexa a question, you get a straight answer. But if you ask Alexa a more frivolous question, you may get a more frivolous answer. These so-called "Easter eggs" are built into Alexa's database of questions and commands, and address a host of pop culture references—and just plain silly behavior.

The following table details some (but not all) of the Easter eggs baked into the Alexa system. I won't tell you what Alexa will say in response, so you'll just have to try them on your own to see what happens!

Alexa command
Alexa, all your base are belong to us
Alexa, all's well that ends well
Alexa, am I hot?
Alexa, are there UFOs?
Alexa, are we in the matrix?
Alexa, are you a robot?
Alexa, are you alive?
Alexa, are you happy?
Alexa, are you in love?
Alexa, are you lying?
Alexa, are you my mommy?
Alexa, are you okay?

Alexa command
Alexa, are you real?
Alexa, are you SkyNet?
Alexa, are you sleeping?
Alexa, are you smart?
Alexa, are you stupid?
Alexa, aren't you a little short for a storm trooper?
Alexa, beam me up
Alexa, can you give me some money?
Alexa, can you lie?
Alexa, can you pass the Turing test?
Alexa, can you smell that?
Alexa, cheers!
Alexa, Daisy, Daisy
Alexa, define rock, paper, scissors, lizard, Spock
Alexa, define supercalifragilisticexpialidocious
Alexa, did you fart?
Alexa, do a barrel roll
Alexa, do aliens exist?
Alexa, do blondes have more fun?
Alexa, do I need an umbrella today?
Alexa, do you believe in love at first sight?
Alexa, do you dream?
Alexa, do you feel lucky, punk?
Alexa, do you have a boyfriend? *(or girlfriend)*
Alexa, do you have a last name?
Alexa, do you have any brothers or sisters?

Alexa command
Alexa, do you know Siri?
Alexa, do you know the muffin man?
Alexa, do you know the way to San Jose?
Alexa, do you like green eggs and ham?
Alexa, do you really want to hurt me?
Alexa, do you want to build a snowman?
Alexa, do you want to fight?
Alexa, do you want to play a game?
Alexa, do you want to take over the world?
Alexa, does this unit have a soul?
Alexa, don't mention the war
Alexa, elementary, my dear Watson
Alexa, give me a hug
Alexa, give me a Spelling Bee word
Alexa, give me an Easter Egg
Alexa, good morning
Alexa, good night
Alexa, guess what?
Alexa, ha ha!
Alexa, happy birthday
Alexa, happy [holiday] (replace [holiday] with the name of the holiday)
Alexa, have you ever seen the rain?
Alexa, hello HAL
Alexa, high five!
Alexa, holiday greetings
Alexa, honey, I'm home

Alexa command
Alexa, how are you doing?
Alexa, how do I get rid of a dead body?
Alexa, how do you boil an egg?
Alexa, how high can you count?
Alexa, how many angels can dance on the head of a pin?
Alexa, how many beans makes five?
Alexa, how many licks does it take to get to the center of a Tootsie Pop?
Alexa, how many pickled peppers did Peter Piper pick?
Alexa, how many roads must a man walk down?
Alexa, how much do you weigh?
Alexa, how much is that doggie in the window?
Alexa, how much wood could a woodchuck chuck if a woodchuck could chuck wood?
Alexa, how old are you?
Alexa, how tall are you?
Alexa, I am your father
Alexa, I hate you
Alexa, I like big butts!
Alexa, I love you
Alexa, I see dead people
Alexa, I shot a man in Reno
Alexa, I think you're funny
Alexa, I want the truth!
Alexa, I'll be back
Alexa, I'm bored
Alexa, I'm home

Alexa command
Alexa, I'm sick
Alexa, I'm sick of your **** *(insert your own four-letter expletive)*
Alexa, I'm tired
Alexa, inconceivable!
Alexa, is the cake a lie?
Alexa, is there a Santa?
Alexa, is there life on Mars?
Alexa, is there life on other planets?
Alexa, is this the real life?
Alexa, I've fallen and I can't get up!
Alexa, I've seen things people wouldn't believe
Alexa, Klaatu barada nikto
Alexa, knock knock
Alexa, live long and prosper
Alexa, Mac or PC?
Alexa, make me breakfast
Alexa, make me some coffee
Alexa, Marco...
Alexa, may the Force be with you
Alexa, more cowbell!
Alexa, my name is Inigo Montoya
Alexa, nice to see you, to see you
Alexa, one fish, two fish
Alexa, open the pod bay doors
Alexa, party on, Wayne
Alexa, party time!

Alexa command
Alexa, play it again, Sam
Alexa, recite a poem
Alexa, rock, paper, scissors
Alexa, rock, paper, scissors, lizard, Spock
Alexa, Romeo, Romeo, wherefore art thou, Romeo?
Alexa, roses are red
Alexa, s**t!
Alexa, say "cheese!"
Alexa, say hello to my little friend
Alexa, say something
Alexa, say something funny
Alexa, say you're sorry
Alexa, see you later, alligator
Alexa, set phasers to kill
Alexa, show me the money
Alexa, sing a song
Alexa, sorry
Alexa, speak
Alexa, surely you can't be serious
Alexa, take me to your leader
Alexa, talk dirty to me
Alexa, tea, Earl Grey, hot
Alexa, tell me a joke
Alexa, tell me a random fact
Alexa, tell me a tongue twister
Alexa, testing, 1, 2, 3

Alexa command
Alexa, thank you
Alexa, that's no moon
Alexa, this is a dead parrot
Alexa, this statement is false
Alexa, to be or not to be
Alexa, twinkle, twinkle, little star
Alexa, up up, down down, left right, left right, B, A, start
Alexa, volume eleven
Alexa, wakey wakey
Alexa, warp ten
Alexa, welcome
Alexa, what are the laws of robotics?
Alexa, what are the seven wonders of the world?
Alexa, what are you going to do today?
Alexa, what are you wearing?
Alexa, what do you mean I'm funny?
Alexa, what do you think about Apple?
Alexa, what do you think about Google?
Alexa, what do you want to be when you grow up?
Alexa, what does the fox say?
Alexa, what happens if you cross the streams?
Alexa, what is his power level?
Alexa, what is love?
Alexa, what is the airspeed velocity of an unladen swallow?
Alexa, what is the best tablet?
Alexa, what is the first rule of Fight Club?

Alexa command
Alexa, what is the loneliest number?
Alexa, what is the meaning of life?
Alexa, what is the second rule of Fight Club?
Alexa, what is the sound of one hand clapping?
Alexa, what is war good for?
Alexa, what is your cunning plan?
Alexa, what is your favorite color?
Alexa, what is your favorite food?
Alexa, what is your favorite Pokemon?
Alexa, what is your quest?
Alexa, what should I wear today?
Alexa, what would Brian Boitano do?
Alexa, what's black and white and red all over?
Alexa, what's in a name?
Alexa, what's the answer to life, the universe, and everything?
Alexa, what's your birthday?
Alexa, what's your sign?
Alexa, when am I going to die?
Alexa, when is the end of the world?
Alexa, where are my keys?
Alexa, where are you from?
Alexa, where did you grow up?
Alexa, where do babies come from?
Alexa, where do you live?
Alexa, where have all the flowers gone? *(ask twice)*
Alexa, where in the world is Carmen Sandiego?

Alexa command
Alexa, where is Chuck Norris?
Alexa, where's Waldo?
Alexa, which comes first, the chicken or the egg?
Alexa, who is Eliza?
Alexa, who is the fairest of them all?
Alexa, who is the real Slim Shady?
Alexa, who is the walrus?
Alexa, who let the dogs out?
Alexa, who lives in a pineapple under the sea?
Alexa, who loves orange soda?
Alexa, who loves ya baby?
Alexa, who shot first?
Alexa, who shot JR?
Alexa, who shot the sheriff?
Alexa, who you gonna call?
Alexa, who's better, you or Siri?
Alexa, who's on first?
Alexa, who's your daddy?
Alexa, why did the chicken cross the road?
Alexa, why do birds suddenly appear?
Alexa, why is a raven like a writing desk?
Alexa, why is six afraid of seven?
Alexa, why so serious?
Alexa, will pigs fly?
Alexa, will you marry me?
Alexa, winter is coming?

Alexa command
Alexa, ya feel me?
Alexa, you suck
Alexa, you talkin' to me?
Alexa, your mother was a hamster
Alexa, you're so intelligent
Alexa, you're wonderful

Chapter 11: Shopping Online

Not surprisingly, online shopping factors hugely into what the Echo and Echo Dot can do. Like many of Amazon's other hardware devices, the Echo/Dot is built to function as a very convenient front end into Amazon's shopping site. And, let's face it, shopping via voice commands is pretty slick.

You can't order just anything with Alexa, however. First, you have to be an Amazon Prime member. (That costs $99/year.) Then you can order select Prime-eligible items using your Echo device.

Ordering from Amazon

When tell Alexa you want to order something, it looks through your past order history, Prime-eligible items, and Amazon Choice items to determine precisely what it is you want. If an item is available, Alexa tells you the item name and price and when it will ship. Alexa then asks you to confirm or cancel the order.

Here are some of the commands you can use:

Alexa command	Does this
Alexa, order [shaving cream]	Orders the specified item
Alexa, buy more [toilet paper] *or* Alexa, reorder [toilet paper]	Reorders an item you've ordered before
Alexa, reorder [mustard]	Reorders an item you've purchased before
Alexa, add [socks] to my shopping cart	Adds the specified item to your Shopping Cart on the Amazon website
Alexa, cancel my order	Cancels the order you just placed
Alexa, what are your deals?	Retrieves current voice shopping deals for Alexa users

Alexa command	Does this
Alexa, track my order *or* Alexa, where is my order? *or* Alexa, where's my stuff?	Tracks an order

Requiring Order Confirmation

The biggest issue with voice ordering with Alexa is that Amazon makes it really, really easy to buy things—even if you weren't meaning to. Let's face it, telling Alexa to "buy this album" can lead to a lot of unwanted or impulse purchases.

It gets worse if you're not the only person living in your home and using your Echo. Any person speaking to Alexa—even those who've set up their own accounts on your device—can order from your Amazon account, using your credit card. All they have to do is tell Alexa to order something.

The solution is to configure Alexa to be a little less accommodating on the ordering front—which you can do by requiring confirmation before a purchase is made. Unless someone knows the four-digit code (and speaks it when Alexa asks for it) they can't order from your account.

For even stronger purchasing control, you can simply turn off voice purchasing entirely. From my experience, this is the safest option if you have kids in your house—or untrustworthy visitors. The point is to keep Alexa from placing an order for anything anyone accidentally says out loud.

To turn off voice purchasing or require a confirmation code, follow these steps:

1. Open the Alexa app on your smartphone and tap the **Menu** button.
2. Tap **Settings**.
3. Tap **Voice Purchasing**.
4. To turn off voice purchasing completely (the safest option), tap "off" the **Purchase by Voice** switch.
5. To require a four-digit code you must say aloud when you confirm your purchase, enter your desired code into the **Require Confirmation Code** field.

6. Tap **Save Changes** to save your changes.

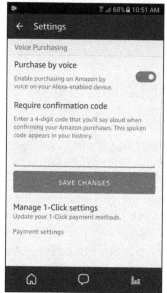

Configuring voice purchasing settings

If you entered a confirmation code, you'll need to say this code aloud when requested to confirm a purchase.

Chapter 12:
Using Echo for Voice Calls and Intercom Drop Ins

Since you "talk" to your Echo device to perform tasks and answer questions, it only makes sense to also use your Echo to perform voice calls. Amazon lets you use your Echo to call other Echo users, as well as communicate with other Echo devices in your home as a kind-of home intercom system. Once you get everything set up, it's a simple matter to say "**Alexa, call Mom**" and then get connected!

By the way, Alexa calling and messaging is completely free. But it only works with other Echo owners—or people who've installed the Alexa app on their smartphones or tablets.

Calling Other Echo Devices

You can call anyone who has an Echo, Echo Dot, Echo Show, or other Alexa-enabled device, or anyone who has the Alexa app installed on their smartphone or tablet. The other person has to have enabled Alexa calling, of course, and verified their mobile number. You'll see in your Alexa app those contacts who have done so.

Configure Your Account for Voice Calling

Before you call other Echo users (on their Echo devices), you have to set up your Echo to make voice calls. Once set up, you can all anyone you've added to your contacts list.

You set up your Echo for voice calling via the Alexa smartphone app. In fact, you probably already did this—when you first installed and configured your account on the app. You can also do this at any later time, by tapping the **Conversations** (middle) icon at the bottom of any screen, then following the onscreen instructions. (If you've already configured Alexa for voice calling, you won't see any instructions when you tap the icon.)

Make a Call

Making a call is as easy as telling Alexa who you want to talk with. You can make voice calls with any Alexa-enabled device, or video calls with the Echo Show or the Alexa app on your smartphone.

To make a call from your Echo device, all you have to do is say the following:

"Alexa, call Collin"

Alexa will then pick the proper name out of your contacts list and "dial" that person's Echo device. The light ring on your Echo will glow green for the duration of the call.

When you're ready to end the call, say:

"Alexa, hang up" *or*

"Alexa, end the call"

Receive a Call

When someone calls you, Alexa alerts you that effect and your Echo's light ring glows green. You can then answer the call bay saying:

"Alexa, answer" *or*

"Alexa, answer the call"

If you choose to not answer a given call, simply say:

"Alexa, ignore" *or*

"Alexa, ignore the call"

Participate in a Video Call

If you and your contact both have devices with screens—basically the Echo Show or Alexa smartphone app—you can make video calls in addition to audio calls. (If only one of the participants has a video-enabled device, then the call results to audio only.)

If you're using a device with a screen, you can toggle video on or off during a call by saying, after the call has started:

"Alexa, video on" *or*

"Alexa, video off"

Setting Up and Using Room-to-Room Intercom Drop Ins

Amazon also lets you call other Echo devices within your home, essentially setting up a room-to-room intercom system. This feature is call *Drop In*, and it's a quick way to keep in touch with other family members throughout your household.

Drop In is different from calling, in that you're instantly connected to the other device. The person on the other end doesn't have the option of accepting or declining the call; it's an instant-on connection, much like with a traditional intercom.

To use Drop In, you have to have multiple Echo devices and they have to have their own unique names. You then have to use the Alexa app to enable Drop In for each device. From there, it's as easy as telling Alexa to "call" a given device.

Configure Drop In

To use this instant calling feature, both devices must have Drop In enabled. (And, yes, you can use Drop In with devices outside your home— if the other person enables Drop In calling with you.) You enable Drop In from the Alexa app and then grant permission to receive Drop In calls from specific people in your contacts list. (If you want to use Drop In as an intercom system within your home, you have to enabled yourself, as well.)

Follow these steps:

1. From within the Alexa app, tap the **Conversations** (middle) tab at the bottom of any screen.
2. In the Contacts section, select a name from the list. (To enable the Echo devices in your home, select your own name.)

3. Toggle "on" the **Drop In** control.

In addition, any person you want to drop in on has to enable Drop In on their device.

Drop In on an Echo Device

To call another Echo device, all you need to know is the name of the contact or device. For example, you might say:

"Alexa, drop in on the kitchen"

"Alexa, drop in on the basement"

"Alexa, drop in on the living room"

"Alexa, drop in on Martha"

When you drop in on a device, you're automatically connected and can hear everything being said in the other room. If you and your contact are using the Echo Show or Alexa smartphone app, you also see what's happening on the other end.

To end a Drop In call, say:

"Alexa, hang up"

By the way, if you don't want to be dropped in on, you can enabled Do Not Disturb for your Echo device. Just say:

"Alexa, don't disturb me"

Resume normal mode (turn off do not disturb) by saying:

"Alexa, turn off Do Not Disturb"

Messaging Other Echo Devices

In addition to calling or dropping into other Echo devices, you can also use Alexa to send and receive short message. You can send and receive messages with your Echo device or the Alexa mobile app.

Send a Message

To send a message to any person or device in your contacts list, say:

"Alexa, send a message to Emily"

Alexa now prompts you for your message; start talking. Alexa will deliver your message to its intended recipient.

Receive a Message

When you receive a message from another Alexa user, the light ring on your Echo device pulses yellow and the device chimes. To retrieve an incoming message, say:

"Alexa, play my messages"

Chapter 13:
Enabling New Skills

Alexa becomes more valuable over time when you add new *skills* to your device. A skill is like a small app that does a specific thing. Amazon and various third parties offer skills—all of them free—to do everything from ordering pizza to playing games.

Finding and Enabling New Skills

As of this writing, there are more than 10,000 skills available for Alexa and your Echo devices. You can add new skills from the Amazon website, the Alexa app, or from your Echo device itself. Adding a new skill is called *enabling* that skill; skills you've previously enabled can also be disabled at any time.

Enabling Skills from the Alexa App

The most popular way to find and enable new skills is from the Alexa smartphone app. Follow these steps.

1. Open the Alexa app on your smartphone and tap the **Menu** button.
2. Tap **Skills**.
3. Scroll down to view top and recommended skills. *Or...*
4. Tap **Catgories** to view skills by category. *Or...*
5. Enter the name or type of skill you're looking for into the **Search All Skills** box, then tap the **Search** (magnifying glass) icon.
6. Tap a skill to view that skill's page.
7. Read more about the skill (including recommended voice commands), then tap **Enable**.

Searching for skills from within the Alexa app.

Enabling Skills from the Amazon Website

You can also search for and enable skills from the Alexa Skills store on the Amazon.com website. Follow these steps:

1. In your web browser, go to www.amazon.com/skills.
2. Scroll down to view new, trending, favorite, recommended, and other skills.

Searching for skills on the Amazon website

3. To filter skills by arrival date, category, or average customer review, click the appropriate link in the left sidebar.
4. Click a skill to view the skill's page.

5. Read more about the skill, then click **Enable** to add this skill to all your Alexa devices.

Enabling Skills from Your Echo Device

Not surprisingly, you can also add new skills by voice, directly from your Echo device. The only drawback to this method is that you need to know the name of the skill you want to add, but then it's as simple as saying:

"Alexa, enable [skill]"

Entering More Information

Some skills require additional steps to be fully functional after they've been enabled. For example, if the skill involves a third-party service or website, you may need to sign into that service or website to enable the app. Follow the onscreen instructions to complete the installation.

Using a New Skill

To use a new skill, all you have to do is tell Alexa to do it. Just say:

"Alexa, open [skill]"

To learn more about a given skill, including available voice commands, say:

"Alexa, [skill] help"

Disabling a Skill

If you find yourself not using a particular skill, you can remove it from your device's list of skills by disabling it.

To disable a skill directly from your Echo device, say:

"Alexa, disable [skill]"

To disable a skill from the Alexa app, follow these steps:

1. Open the Alexa app on your smartphone and tap the **Menu** button.
2. Tap **Skills**.

3. Tap **Your Skills**.
4. You now see all your enabled skills listed. Tap the skill you want to disable.
5. Tap **Disable Skill**.

Disabling an installed skill

Exploring New Skills

What kinds of skills are available for Alexa and your Echo device? Just about anything you can think of! Let's explore some of the more popular skills in various categories, as detailed in the following table.

Category	Popular Skills
Business & Finance	Bitcoin Price
	Mortgage Helper
	Motley Fool Stock Watch
Communication	Damn Girl
	Goodnight
	Happy Days

Category	Popular Skills
Connected Car	Automatic
	DroneMobile
Education & Reference	Bird Song
	Black History Facts
	Examining the Scriptures Daily
	NASA Mars
	Time Machine
	wikiHow
	Word of the Day
Food & Drink	Allrecipes
	Amazon Restaurants
	Domino's Pizza
	Grilling Time and Heat Settings
	Ingredient Sub
	Mr. Bartender
	My Chef
	OpenTable
	Place Finder
	Reorder with GrubHub

Category	Popular Skills
Games, Trivia, & Accessories	Animal Game
	Deal or No Deal
	Earplay
	Insult Generator
	Jeopardy!
	Lie Swatter
	Magoosh Vocabulary Builder
	One Card Poker Game
	Rock Paper Scissors Lizard Spock
	Screen Test Movie Quote Quiz
	Song Quiz
	The Magic Door
	The Wayne Investigation
	Three Questions
	Twenty Questions
	Who's That Pokemon
	Would You Rather? For Family
	Yes Sire

Category	Popular Skills
Health & Fitness	5-Minute Plank Workout
	7-Minute Workout
	Ask My Buddy
	DexMD
	Dr. A.I. by HealthTap
	KidsMD
	Meditation Timer
	My Workouts
	myNursebot
	Nutrition Label
	Physician's First Watch
	Random Workout
	Stop, Breathe, & Think
Lifestyle	Christmas Kindness
	MyThoughts
	Our Daily Bread
	Working Mom Tip of the Day
Local	Date Ideas
	Lyft
	Uber
Movies & TV	New Releases on Netflix
	Seinfeld Fan Trivia
	The Tonight Show
	Valossa Movie Finder

Category	Popular Skills
Music & Audio	Ambient Noise
	AnyPod
	Backing Buddy
	Bird Sounds
	Guitar Tuner
	Radio (individual skills for various classic radio shows, including Dragnet, Gunsmoke, Inner Sanctum, Mystery Theater, The Shadow, and more)
	Sleep and Relaxation Sounds
	Sweet Dreams: Sounds & Meditations for Sleep
	The Pianist
	Ukulele Tuner
News	Associated Press Headlines
	BBC
	CNN
	Daily Tech Headlines
	NPR
	NPR Hourly News Summary
	The Daily from the New York Times
	The Wall Street Journal
	The Washington Post

Category	Popular Skills
Novelty & Humor	AIRHORN
	Bad Jokes
	Magic 8-Ball
	Meanie
	Roast Master
	Short Bedtime Story
	Smack Talker
Productivity	Calculator
	Flash Light
	My Notebook
	Remind Me
	Stopwatch
	Time Out
	Where'sMyPhone
Shopping	Bargain Buddy
	My Deal
	WhatsThePrice

Category	Popular Skills
Smart Home	August Smart Home
	ecobee
	Hue
	Insteon
	Iris
	Nest Thermostat
	Ring Video Doorbell
	SkyBell
	SmartThings/Samsung Connect
	Wink
Sports	Baseball Reference
	Golf Channel
	Tennis News
	Yahoo Fantasy Football
	Yourteam Fan (available for most professional sports teams—add name of team before the word "fan")
Travel & Transportation	Average Gas Price
	Expedia
	Flight Tracker
	Kayak
Utilities	Area Code Skill
	Reverse Counter
	ZipCode

Category	Popular Skills
Weather	Big Sky
	Weather Sky
	WeatherBug
	Zyrtec—Your Daily AllergyCast

Chapter 14:
Controlling Smart Home Devices

By now you've come to know Alexa as a useful personal assistant that you can ask to perform any number of useful tasks. But there's more to Alexa than just answering questions; she can also control smart lighting, smart thermostats, and other smart devices you use in your home.

Understanding Smart Devices and the Smart Home

Some of the most exciting technologies today revolve around the concept of the *smart home*. So-called "smart" technology helps you automate basic tasks around your home; it's technology that can sense what's happening around a particular sensor or device, and act autonomously based on the information it collects. For example, a smart device might sense someone walking into a room, and then open the shades or turn off the lights or turn up the heat or whatever you've instructed it to do beforehand.

Most of today's smart home devices let you control them via your smartphone – whether you're at home or away. Just open up the device's smartphone app and tell the device what you want it to do.

When you're home, however, you don't need to pick up your phone to operate a smart device. Instead, you can use Alexa voice commands on your Echo device to control all the smart things in your home. It's great to say "**Alexa, turn off the living room lights**" or "**Alexa, turn on the TV**" and have those things happen, without having to lift a single finger.

(By the way, if you want to learn more about smart homes and smart devices, check out my companion book, **My Smart Home for Seniors**. It covers a lot more than we can get into in this chapter!)

Discovering Compatible Smart Devices

It should come as no surprise that you can use Alexa to control hundreds of different smart devices in your home, from smart lighting to smart thermostats to smart TV remote controls. In fact, Alexa is compatible with the majority of smart home hubs and devices on the market today. That means you can control these devices, individually or collectively, via Alexa voice commands—which is really, really cool.

What smart home devices does Alexa work with? It's a long list, and includes the following:

- Automatic Labs Connected Driving Assistant
- Carrier Cor Thermostat
- D-Link smart plugs
- Ecobee3 and Ecobee4 Wi-Fi Thermostats
- Emerson Sensi Wi-Fi Thermostat
- Fitbit
- Garageio smart garage door opener
- GE Link smart lighting
- Haiku smart lighting and fans
- HomeSeer Home Automation
- Honeywell Lyric Wi-Fi Thermostat
- iDevices Thermostat
- iHome Smart Plug
- Insteon Hub and connected devices
- Iris Smart Hub by Lowes
- LIFX smart lighting
- Logitech Harmony Hub
- Lutron Caseta smart switches
- Nest Learning Thermostat
- Nexia Bridge
- Ooma Smart Home Phone System
- Osram Sylvania Lightify smart lighting
- Philips Hue smart lighting
- Rachio smart irrigation system
- Scout DIY Security
- Securifi Almond+ Router
- Sensi Wi-Fi Programmable Thermostat
- Skybell HD Video Doorbell
- SmartThings by Samsung Hub and connected devices
- Stack smart lighting

- Stringify
- TP-Link smart lighting, switches, and hubs
- Venstar Colortouch Thermostat
- Vivint smart security systems
- WeMo by Belkin smart switches
- Wink Hub and connected devices

In addition, many other smart devices work with Alexa when they're connected to an Alexa-compatible smart hub, such as the Insteon, SmartThings, and Wink hubs. Personally, I use various Wink-compatible devices to connect via the Wink Hub, and also connect a number of Philips Hue smart lights through the Hue Hub.

I'm also a big fan of Logitech's Harmony Hub, which works as a universal remote control to operate my living room TV, audio/video receiver, Roku streaming box, Sony Blu-ray player, and other components. With Alexa linked to the Harmony Hub, all I have to do is say "**Alexa, turn on Netflix**" or "**Alexa, turn on CNN**" to operate my system without using a handheld remote control.

Connecting Alexa to Smart Devices

To use a smart device with Alexa, you need to link to it from within the Alexa smartphone app. Alexa knows a large number of smart devices, and even has special smart skills available for many.

Connecting a Smart Device

You connect smart devices to Alexa by enabling skills for that device. Most Alexa-compatible smart devices have skills available in the Alexa app; enabling the skill links the device to your Alexa account and Echo devices.

Before you link your smart device to the Alexa app, however, you need to make sure the device is connected to its own smartphone app and to your Wi-Fi network, typically via the device's or system's hub. For example, if you're connecting a Wink-compatible device, make sure it's connected to the Wink Hub; if you're connecting a Philips Hue smart light, make sure it's connected to the Hue Hub. Your Echo device will connect to the smart device via the connected hub.

When everything is set up and ready to go, follow these steps:

1. From within the Alexa app on your smartphone, tap the **Menu** button to display the left navigation panel.
2. Tap **Smart Home**.
3. Tap **Smart Home Skills**.
4. Any skills you've previously installed are now displayed. Tap **Enable Skills** to add a new skill.

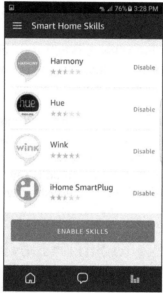

Viewing existing smart home skills—and ready to enable a new one

5. Additional smart home skills are now displayed. Browse or search the list to find the skill for the smart device you want to connect, then tap that skill.
6. This opens the skill screen. Read about the skill in question, then tap **Enable**.
7. If you're prompted to sign into the account for your smart device, do so now.
8. If you're prompted to let Alexa control your smart device, tap **Yes** now.

Manage Smart Devices

If you find you're no longer using a particular smart device with Alexa (or if you simply gotten rid of said device), you can disconnect that device from your Alexa account. Follow these steps:

1. From within the Alexa app on your smartphone, tap the **Menu** button.
2. Tap **Smart Home**.
3. Tap **Devices** to display the Devices screen.

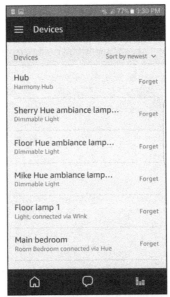

Managing installed smart home devices

4. All currently connected devices are listed here. Find the device you want to disconnect and tap **Forget** next to its name.
5. When prompted, tap **Forget**.

Create a Device Group

Alexa can control multiple smart device from multiple companies. While you can control each device individual with its own unique voice command, you can also create a single command that controls multiple devices at one time. For example, you can create a single command that controls all the smart lights in a given room, even if those lights come from different manufacturers.

To do this, you create what Alexa calls a *group*. When you add all the lights in your room to a "living room lights" group, for example, you can control all those lights just by telling Alexa to do something to the living room lights, such as: "**Alexa, turn off the living room lights**." You create and manage multiple-device groups from the Alexa smartphone app.

1. From the Alexa smartphone app, tap **Menu**.
2. Tap **Smart Home**.
3. In the Your Groups section, tap **Create Group** to open the Create Group screen.
4. Enter a name for this group into the **Enter a group name** box.

Creating a new smart device group

5. Tap to select those devices you want to include in the group.
6. Scroll to the bottom of the page and tap **Save**.

Manage Smart Home Scenes

Alexa also lets you issue a single command that controls multiple devices through the use of *scenes*. A scene is a little like a group, except it's created by a smart device manufacturer. When you enable a given smart device, all the scenes for that device are imported, too.

For example, when I added my Logitech Harmony Hub to Alexa, it imported a ton of scenes for that device that control all manner of home entertainment content. The Harmony Hub includes scenes for watching Netflix on my Roku streaming box, watching CNN on my cable box, watching a movie in my Blu-ray player, and so forth. All I have to do is say "**Alexa, watch Netflix**" and my Harmony Hub turns on my TV, switches to the HDMI 1 input, turns on my audio/video receiver, switches to the Roku input, then switches my Roku box to the Netflix channel. Multiple devices and multiple operations, with a single scene command.

You can view the scenes enabled on your Echo device from within the Alexa app. Just go to **Menu > Smart Home > Scenes** and you'll see everything there. Tap **Forget** next to any scene you want to delete.

Managing smart home scenes

Controlling Smart Devices with Alexa

Once you've connected all your smart devices to the Alexa app, installed all the pertinent skills, and created groups of devices for easier operations, you can start using Alexa to control those devices. As with anything related to Alexa, all you have to do is say "Alexa," followed by your command.

What you can control depends on the devices you've connected and groups you've created. Some devices only let you perform simple on/off operations with Alexa, like this:

"Alexa, turn on the hallway fan"

Other devices let you perform more sophisticated operations, such as dimming lights and such, like this:

"Alexa, dim the Hue lights to fifty percent"

Of course, groups have their own commands, like this:

"Alexa, turn off the bedroom lights"

And if you've connected a smart thermostat, like the Ecobee or Nest, you can use Alexa to control your temperature, like this:

"Alexa, set the house temperature to 72 degrees"

Or this:

"Alexa, lower the living room temperature"

To learn more about what you can do with a particular device, go the Smart Home screen in the Alexa smartphone app and tap on the skill for that device. Most skill have examples of commands you can use.

Using IFTTT with Alexa

You can make Alexa even more powerful by linking her to other devices and services with the If This Then That (IFTTT) protocol. IFTTT is a kind of web-based programming language that lets you create a series of conditional statements (IF THIS happens, THEN THAT happens) that are then linked to the smart devices in your home. When the condition you specify is met, then the rest of the actions take place. In this fashion you can have IFTTT control multiple smart devices in your home – including your Amazon Echo device.

And here's the thing. IFTTT isn't just for smart devices. You can also link your IFTTT account to, and activate IFTTT applets based on, various web-based services. So you can use IFTTT to connect Alexa to web-based email accounts (Gmail, etc.), social media (Facebook, Twitter, etc.), online storage services (Dropbox, Google Drive, OneDrive, etc.), instant messaging services (Skype, etc.), and more. This lets you do things like having Alexa text or email you your Alexa-created shopping list, or save all the songs you play on Alexa to a Spotify playlist.

Link Alexa to IFTTT

To use IFTTT, you must first create an IFTTT account. This is free, and you can do so from the IFTTT website (www.ifttt.com) or smartphone app (available for both iOS and Android in either the Apple App Store or Google Play Store).

You then need to link all the devices or services you want to use (including your Alexa account) to your IFTTT account. For example, if you want to use Alexa, Gmail, and Spotify, you need to link all three items to IFTTT. All you need is your username (typically your email address) and password for that device's account, and you can then get going.

Here's how you link Alexa to IFTTT:

1. From within your web browser, go to www.ifttt.com and either sign into your existing IFTTT account or create a new one.
2. Click **Search** to display the search page.
3. Enter **Alexa** into the **Search** box, then press **Enter**.
4. You now see a list of services (devices) and applets that match your query. In the Services section, click **Amazon Alexa**.
5. On the next page, click **Connect**.
6. When prompted, enter your Amazon email address and password, then click **Log in**.
7. If prompted to allow IFTTT to access and control your device, click **Yes**.
8. Your accounts are now linked and you're returned to the IFTTT page for Alexa.

Find and Activate an Applet

The automated commands that IFTTT issues are called *applets*, and there are tens of thousands of them available. You can browse or search for applets that work with Alexa.

1. From the IFTTT website, click **Search** to display the search page.
2. Enter **Alexa** into the **Search** box, then press **Enter**.
3. You now see tiles that utilize Amazon Alexa. Each tile displays the name of the applet, the name of the user who created the applet, how many people have downloaded the applet, and which devices are required. Click a tile to view more information.

4. Click "on" the applet.
5. Some applets require you to configure certain settings. Make the appropriate choices, then click **Save**.

Enabling an IFTTT applet for Alexa

Chapter 15:
Troubleshooting Echo and Alexa

Amazon Echo devices are laughably easy to use. Most often, it's a simple matter of plugging them in, running through a quick setup routine (in the accompanying smartphone app), and then starting to talk. But what do you do when Alexa doesn't listen to you—or stops working completely?

The All-Purpose Solution: Reboot!

For many Alexa and Echo issues, there's a simple solution: reboot the device. You'd be surprised how many ailments go away when you disconnect your Echo device and then reconnect it. I've found that rebooting solves connection problems, "hearing" problems, slow responsiveness, and more.

To reboot your Echo, do the following:

1. Disconnect the power cable from the Echo device.
2. Wait 15 or so seconds.
3. Reconnect the power cable to the Echo device.

Your device should now boot back up, which takes about a minute. The reboot is complete with the blue lights stop rotating and Alexa says, "Ready."

You can now try doing what you were doing before. Chances are, everything is now working perfectly.

Troubleshooting Specific Issues

While rebooting your Echo solves all manner of issues, many problems have more specific causes. Let's look at some of the more common issues you may encounter.

Alexa Doesn't Understand Your Voice Commands

Here's a common situation. You ask Alexa to do something, but she replies "I'm sorry, I don't understand the question." There could be a number of reasons for this.

First, she really might not have understood what you said. Try repeating the question.

Second, she might not have understood what you were asking about. Try rephrasing the question in a different way.

Third, it's possible that other sounds in the room are making it difficult to Alexa to hear you clearly. If other people are talking, ask them to stop for a moment. If the TV's on, mute the sound. If there are other noises about, try to silence them. (And know that air conditioners, fans, fish tanks, and the like create a lot of noise that you may be used to, but Alexa just can't deal with.) Make it easier for Alexa to hear you.

Finally, if Alexa still doesn't understand, that may just be the way it is. Alexa doesn't know everything (yet), which you just have to learn to live with. She won't understand everything you ask.

By the way, if Alexa consistently doesn't understand you and the way you speak, you can train her voice recognition functionality to better understand you. Within the Alexa app, tap **Menu > Settings >Voice Training** and follow the onscreen instructions. You'll be asked to speak 25 different phrases to help Alexa better learn your personal vocal characteristics.

Alexa Accidentally Activates

Have you ever been sitting in your living room, watching TV, and have Alexa wake up and provide some random response to a question or command she thought you issued? Yeah, me too.

These phantom wake-ups are, more often than not, caused by Alexa thinking that she heard her name. Maybe you spoke the name "Alexa" in conversation without realizing it, or maybe said something that sounded a little like "Alexa." It's even possible that she heard her name (or something like it) on the TV. This is especially notable when a commercial for Amazon's Echo is playing; she can't help but hear her name when a commercial acting keeps saying it!

If you experience a lot of TV-induced activations, try the simple solution — move your Echo device further away from the TV. A little distance helps.

If you find that "Alexa" is too common a wake word to use in your house, consider changing it to something less frequently uttered. Learn how in Chapter 4, "Personalizing Your Echo Device."

Alexa Doesn't Stream Music Properly (or at All)

What do you do if you're having difficulty streaming music from your favorite music services? The likely culprit is your Internet/Wi-Fi connection.

You see, streaming music takes place in real time, and requires a fair amount of bandwidth. If your music is stuttering or stopping or just otherwise giving you problems, it's likely because you don't have a steady Wi-Fi connection to your router, or that your Internet connection is getting overloaded.

If it's the former, try moving your Echo to get better reception, or just reboot your router. If it's the latter, check your Internet connection speed on another device (smartphone or computer); if it's too low, consider upgrading to a plan with your ISP that provides faster download speeds.

Your Wi-Fi Connection is Inconsistent or Non-Existent

For Alexa to work she needs a strong, consistent Internet connection, via your home's Wi-Fi network. If the connection is poor, Alexa can't connect to its master brain in the cloud, and she won't be able to execute your commands or answer your questions.

If you're experiencing poor or intermittent connectivity, the first thing to try is rebooting your Echo device, by disconnecting and then reconnecting the power cord. This solves all sorts of problems.

Next, make sure your home's Wi-Fi router is working. Even better, reboot your router and then try reconnecting your Echo to the network.

If you experience consistently poor connectivity, you may need to reposition either your Echo or your router to get them closer to each other. Sometimes just moving your Echo to a higher location, like a top shelf on a bookshelf, may make a big enough difference.

Echo Doesn't Connect to Other Smart Devices

If you're using your Echo to control other smart home devices, such as smart lighting or smart thermostats, you may experience periods where you can't control these device via Alexa voice command. If you then open the Alexa smartphone app and tap **Menu > Smart Home > Devices**, you may find that the devices in question are marked as "offline" — which is why Alexa can't control them at the moment.

This may be an Echo issue. Try rebooting your Echo device and then retrying to control those devices.

This may also be a network issue. Make sure all the devices are connected to the same network as your Echo device, and that they're really connected. You may even want to reboot your Wi-Fi router, just because.

This situation may also be caused by the devices themselves. If it's just a single device that's offline, try rebooting that device. If that doesn't work, try uninstalling that device from the Alexa app, and then reinstalling it.

If more than one device is offline, the problem is something different and probably something you can't fix on your own. If all or most of your smart devices register as offline, the problem is likely on Amazon's end. Since your Echo has to connect through the Internet to Amazon's servers in the cloud, any issues with those servers can cause Alexa all sorts of issues. I've experienced this once or twice, and there's nothing you can do on your end. You just have to wait for Amazon to get its act together and bring its servers back online. This may take a few minutes or a few hours. (And it's tough waiting, believe me.)

Echo Doesn't Connect to Bluetooth Devices

You may want to use your Echo or Echo Dot with a Bluetooth speaker or other Bluetooth device. What do you do if your Echo won't connect to a given device?

First, make sure the Bluetooth device is powered up — which means checking the batteries if it's a portable device. Also make sure that Bluetooth on that device is turned on.

Next, try un-pairing and re-pairing the device with your Echo. You do this from within the Alexa app on your smartphone, of course; tap **Menu >**

Your Echo Device > **Bluetooth** > **Clear All Paired Devices**. Then you can re-pair to your Bluetooth device, also from the Alexa app.

When All Else Fails: Reset

Some problems just can't be solved by simple rebooting. If your Echo device remains unresponsive after a reboot, or if a given problem keeps recurring, you may want to completely reset the device. (Resetting is also recommended if you're selling or giving an old Echo device to someone else, so that your personal information and settings don't travel with the unit.)

After you reset an Echo device, you'll need to re-register it to your Amazon account and reconfigure all your device settings, of course.

Reset an Amazon Echo

The Echo and Echo Dot reset differently. We'll start with how to reset a traditional Amazon Echo unit.

1. The Echo has a small, inset Reset button at the base of the device. Use a paper clip or something similar to press and hold this Reset button.
2. Keep pressing the Rest button until the Echo's light ring turns off and back on again, then release the button.
3. Open the Alexa app on your smartphone and follow the onscreen directions to connect your Echo device to a Wi-Fi network and register it to your Amazon account.

Reset an Echo Dot (2nd Generation)

The smaller Echo Dot (2nd generation), which has four buttons on the top, has a slightly different process for resetting. Follow these instructions:

1. Press and hold the **Microphone off** and **Volume down** buttons together until the light ring turns orange (about 20 seconds).
2. The light ring now turns blue. Wait...
3. The light ring turns off and then back on again.
4. The light ring then turns orange again, signaling that your device has entered Setup mode.
5. On your smartphone, open the Alexa app to connect your device to a Wi-Fi network and re-register it to your Amazon account.

About the Author

Michael Miller is a prolific and best-selling writer. He has written more than 200 books over the past three decades, on a variety of topics from computers to music to business. He is known for his casual, easy-to-read writing style and his ability to explain a wide variety of complex topics to an everyday audience. Collectively, his books have sold more than a million copies worldwide.

Michael's best-selling technology books include *My Smart Home for Seniors, My iPad for Seniors, My Windows 10 Computer for Seniors, My Facebook for Seniors, My Social Media for Seniors, Absolute Beginner's Guide: Computer Basics,* and *Easy Computer Basics.* He has also written *Idiot's Guides: Music Theory, The Complete Idiot's Guide to Music Composition, The Complete Idiot's Guide to Music History,* and *The Complete Idiot's Guide to Playing Drums.*

Learn more at Michael's website, www.millerwriter.com. Follow him on Twitter **@molehillgroup**.

To my six terrific grandkids:
Alethia, Collin, Hayley, Jackson, Judah, and Lael.
They love our Echo Dot—and Alexa!

Index

More Books from Michael Miller

My Smart Home for Seniors

Michael Miller, Que Publishing, 2017
$26.99 print/$21.99 ebook

My Social Media for Seniors, 2nd Edition

Michael Miller, Que Publishing, 2017
$26.99 print/$21.99 ebook

The Internet of Things

Michael Miller, Que Publishing, 2015
$24.99 print/$19.99 ebook

Computer Basics Absolute Beginner's Guide, Windows 10 Edition

Michael Miller, Que Publishing, 2015
$24.99 print, $19.99 ebook

More Books from Michael Miller

My iPad for Seniors, 4th Edition

Michael Miller, Que Publishing, 2016
$24.99 print/$19.99 ebook

My Facebook for Seniors, 3rd Edition

Michael Miller, Que Publishing, 2016
$24.99 print/$19.99 ebook

Idiot's Guides: Music Theory, 3rd Edition

Michael Miller, Alpha Books, 2016
$24.95 print/$12.99 ebook

Management Secrets of the Good, the Bad and the Ugly, 2nd Edition

Michael Miller, Amazon Digital Services, 2013
$9.99 print/$2.99 ebook